IN A NUTSHELL

a manifesto for trees and a guide to growing and protecting them

by

Neil Sinden
with drawings by David Nash
for
COMMON GROUND

Published by Common Ground 1989
45 Shelton Street, London, WC2H 9HJ

ISBN 1 870364 04 X

Typeset and designed on a desk top computer by
Common Ground at Neals Yard DTP Studio, Covent Garden,
London, WC2

Printed by Wincanton Litho, Wincanton, Somerset, on 100%
recycled paper and coverboard - Sylvancoat and Speckletone
(hazel).

IN A NUTSHELL

a manifesto for trees and a guide to growing and protecting them

CONTENTS

3. PROJECTS

4. TREE PROTECTION AND THE LAW

5. ORGANISATIONS CONCERNED WITH TREES

6. SOURCES OF GRANT AID

ACKNOWLEDGEMENTS

The TREES, WOODS AND THE GREEN MAN project has enjoyed financial support from the Department of Environment; the London Boroughs Grants Scheme; the Ernest Cook Trust; the Nature Conservancy Council and a London-based trust.   We are grateful to all these organisations and specifically to the Nature Conservancy Council and the London Boroughs Grants Scheme whose support has made this book possible. Responsibility for the contents rests with Common Ground.

We thank all the groups and individuals - especially Harry Baker, Alan Mitchell, Oliver Rackham and numerous local authority tree officers - who have provided information, clarification and support for the project and book. We would like to thank Heather Harrison and Kathleen Raine for permission to reproduce their poems. We are also extremely grateful to Tony Fuller and Ted Hammond for their enthusiasm and encouragement and to Dr. Keith Kirby for his valued comments on the draft. Special thanks are due to Richard Mabey for the foreword and his constant questions, and answers.

Above all we would like to thank David Nash for his drawings and the enthusiastic response to our exacting requests.

hazel nuts

In A Nutshell

COMMON GROUND

The COMMON GROUND project TREES, WOODS AND THE GREEN MAN aims to heighten awareness not simply of the ecological and economic reliance on trees and woods but also of the value of our long cultural and emotional relationship with them.

We feel that an appreciation of nature and our common cultural heritage is not enough; we must have an active commitment to their conservation. There is no excuse for inaction, We each have a responsibility to care for our own place, and to ensure that its character and distinctiveness is enhanced, not eroded by change.

COMMON GROUND promotes the importance of our common cultural inheritance: everyday nature and buildings, popular history and local places. We do this by exploring and developing links with the arts and encouraging local conservation action emphasising the cultural, aesthetic and emotional bonds that we develop with the places in which we live.

Common Ground's other projects are PARISH MAPS, NEW MILESTONES and LOCAL DISTINCTIVENESS.

Common Ground
45 Shelton Street
London, WC2H 9HJ

IMAGE BY BEN NICHOLSON

FOREWORD by Richard Mabey

Not so many years ago there was talk in planning circles about the possibility of replacing real trees in city centres with replicas made from reinforced plastic. It would, so the theory went, solve a host of municipal problems at a stroke: no more vandalised saplings, no pavements composted by autumn leaves, not one more windthrown branch to damage a ratepayer's car. And fluttering their colour-fast PVC leaves above the traffic, these new urban monuments would still set off the concrete quite splendidly - just like architect's models, in fact.

The suggestion, needless to say, was laughed out of court, for it is precisely the quirkiness that occasionally makes trees a nuisance that also endears them to us. We love them for their liveliness, for their changes through the seasons and through our lives, for their ageing and persistence, for their individuality.

Our attitudes towards trees are full of such paradoxes. They are symbols of life, but also of wilderness, and of all that stands in the way of "civilisation". They are the natural climax vegetation of most of the planet, yet are obstinately viewed, even by their friends, as some kind of human benefaction. And, most ironically, they continue to be destroyed across the globe in barely credible quantities, just at the moment when we are beginning to understand their crucial role in regulating the climate. We say we love them but somehow we have not yet learned how to live together.

IN A NUTSHELL is an attempt to resolve some of these paradoxes. It is a guide to how we might join imaginative response with practical understanding to reach a modus vivendi with trees. It is also a manifesto, suggesting a set of principles which should guide our actions, and which insist on a deeper respect for trees - and a greater confidence, too, that these ancient organisms may have wiser plans than ours about where and how to grow.

For whatever is at fault in our troubled relationship, it would be hard to say that it is the trees that are not pulling their weight. Even in their current depleted numbers they are still the planet's lungs, converting sunlight to living tissue and doing their best to absorb the carbon dioxide with which we are drenching the atmosphere. They will grow entirely by themselves, stabilise soil, purify water, spring up again when blown or cut down - all without any assistance from humans. Over the centuries they help shape the character of the places where they grow, and it takes very determined action to wipe out their traces.

IN A NUTSHELL is full of wise suggestions about how trees can contribute to a community's sense of place. It talks about the role of trees in backyard tubs, in streets, in schools and churchyards and hospital grounds; about parish woods and orchards; about which species are most likely to succeed, and which have the best "fit" for particular landscapes. It discusses how these principles translate into practice, how trees can be grown from seed and cuttings, how and when they should be planted - but also, crucially, how in many places deliberate planting is a poor substitute for simply allowing indigenous trees to spring up of their own accord. As Oliver Rackham has written "Tree-planting is not synonymous with conservation. It is an admission that conservation has failed."

There are sections, too on what is usually called "management" - though this is a term which is out of keeping with the tone of this text. Rather they are about techniques of negotiation with trees, about ways of encouraging their natural settlement and growth inside a context of human needs - both material and spiritual. No where is this more important than in the care of one of Britain's special legacies - its old trees, which are so often dismissed in forestry jargon as "senile" or "overmature".

At its heart IN A NUTSHELL is an exploration of the respective virtues of "naturalness" and "cultivation". It took the Great Storm of October 1987 to remind us of how unsure we still are of our position in this ancient argument. The apparent loss of 15 million trees in a single night unleashed a great fund of previously muted affection. Yet it was an affection that fell some way short of trust.

Trees which were merely fallen or tilted were assumed to be dead, and written off as so much rubbish. An entirely natural disaster, of the kind our woods will have recovered from repeatedly over the centuries, was assumed to be reparable only by human intervention - as if trees were an invention of humankind, or worse, a kind of pet.

COMMON GROUND has always stressed the importance of links between conservation and the arts, and it was sculptors like David Nash (who has contributed the drawings to this book) and Michael Fairfax who began to break down some of these old and arrogant attitudes. They have explored the vitality of fallen trees, looked for new meanings in changed scenes, and above all tried to understand and humanise the process of natural change.

Michael Fairfax's prophetic work "The Trees Rattle Too", a reworking of the idea of the Aeolian harp, survived the storm in its Sussex wood location and propped up two half-fallen oaks in the process - a reminder of the ambivalence of natural forces, and a harbinger of the massive natural regeneration that followed.

John Berger once wrote: "Art does not imitate nature, it imitates a creation, sometimes to propose an alternative world, sometimes simply to amplify, to confirm, to make social the brief hope offered by nature." This is also the intention of IN A NUTSHELL, to make social the hope and example offered by trees.

In A Nutshell

YEW

COMMON GROUND'S MANIFESTO FOR TREES

Trees are the key to our survival. They came before us and we have used, abused and loved them for thousands of years. They have provided our sustenance - food, shelter, medicine and the air we breathe. They are our past and future.

Yet we take them for granted. We cut them down without thinking and we are obsessed with planting, but we forget to care for the tree. Our culture is rich with trees, woods and green men - from pollards and timber barns to paintings and poetry, from the Green Knight and Robin Hood to Constable and Elgar. We urgently need to find new ways of living happily with trees as cultural, spiritual and emotional companions - as well as for ecological reasons.

The advent of global warming, massive forest clearance, and a growing awareness of damage to trees by acid rain and the lowering of water tables makes the need to nurture existing trees an imperative. We can all help in some way. Common Ground urges you to consider how you can implement and expand the following ideas in your own neighbourhood or parish.

1. All trees should be protected

Trees stand for nature, we shall stand or fall with them. Felling a tree should be a last resort when no other options are open to us, although different considerations must form the basis for working woodlands.

The importance of trees to the health of the earth is only just being understood, although their symbolic value in many cultures has been apparent for millennia. Before considering felling a tree we

should ask ourselves:
- if by felling other trees will be given the opportunity to grow and replace it.
- what wild life depends on it
- how people value it.
- if the timber is going to be put to a really worthwhile use.
- if it can't be coppiced or pollarded instead

Many trees are already protected by law and it is illegal to fell a protected tree without permission. Work for the protection of all trees. Make every tree a wanted tree.

2. Stand up for old trees and ancient woodland

All old trees and ancient woodland are priceless and should be jealously guarded. Old trees are more important than young trees, culturally, ecologically and aesthetically. They are a distinguishing characteristic of the British countryside. Despite years of protest we are still losing irreplaceble tracts of ancient woodland at an alarming rate - more than half has been lost in the past 40 years to fields, conifers and development. We are prejudiced against old trees. We call them geriatric and overmature, forgetting that they can happily look that way for hundreds of years. Tree protection law should be biased in favour of old trees - penalties for cutting down or damaging trees should increase with the age of the tree. Remember, for some trees life begins at 400.

3. Keep the carbon locked up

Single trees, small clumps, large standard trees in coppice woods and well-spaced hedgerow trees with large well-developed canopies absorb more carbon than tightly-packed trees. We must allow room for trees to flourish. An acre of American sycamore can absorb 3 tonnes of carbon per year. Wood should not be burnt unnecessarily as it adds to the build-up of carbon dioxide in the atmosphere. We need to find permanent uses for timber harvested from woods so that the carbon is not released thereby increasing the rate of global warming.

4. Recycle paper

Each of us consumes about two tree's worth of paper products every year. The daily circulation of one popular newspaper consumes 4000 trees alone. We currently recycle less than one third of the paper we use in this country - the rest is burnt, releasing carbon into the atmosphere, or goes into expensive, unsightly and dangerous rubbish dumps. We all waste vast amounts. We should use more recycled paper. The quality of these products is improving all the time - the more we use the better it gets. Collect and recycle waste paper at home, in your office, at school and in your neighbourhood.

5. Encourage natural regeneration

Existing woods should be given the opportunity to expand by natural regeneration. We should ensure that current changes in farming policy pay back part of the damage to trees due to years of agricultural expansion. Woodland is an ideal use for surplus farmland and unused land in towns. The simplest and cheapest way to extend woodlands is by fencing-off land adjacent to existing woods to allow seeds to grow up protected from browsing animals.

old ash hedge tree -

6. Get behind the hedge

Hedges and hedgerow trees are historically important in our landscape. Some hedges have marked boundaries for a thousand years and are remnants of ancient woodland. They serve as windbreaks sheltering crops, stock and wild life and reduce soil erosion. But we're losing more hedges than ever before - through the 1980's the rate of hedgerow destruction has continued to accelerate to over 4,000 miles each year. Hedgerows should be protected. Encourage farmers to carry out traditional hedgelaying. Mark hedgerow saplings to save them from hedge cutters. Grow new hedges - even in towns.

7. Grow your own trees

Grow trees from locally-collected seed wherever possible. Many nurseries get their stock from overseas. You may think that you are buying an English oak, a Welsh Yew or a Scots Pine but it might well come from Holland or France. By using seed collected locally you can enhance local distinctiveness and preserve genetic diversity. The resulting trees are likely to adapt better to local soils and climate.

8. Think carefully before you plant a tree

We have an obsession with planting trees yet paradoxically tree planting is an indication of previous and often present shortsightedness. It's as if we need to assert our mastery over nature and it is too easy to bask in the publicity of planting and forget what happens next. Trees are planted without thought for existing trees and saplings or the views of local people. It has been estimated that something like half the newly planted trees in urban areas die within 10 years from lack of care. Look after the trees that are already there and encourage natural regeneration. Trees that have established themselves naturally will grow faster and stronger. If there is no alternative but to plant, choose carefully to reinforce the local mix of trees. In towns however, it may be exciting to create a new personality for an area by planting unusual trees.

9. Grow the right trees in the right place

Different types of tree have associations with different places. Most native trees will grow anywhere but they have preferences for soil, moisture and climate. Alders and willows like wet places; oak does well in heavy clay soils; pines will grow in very exposed situations and beech has become associated with the landscape of chalk downland. We should grow trees around us in the country and in our towns which enhance the identity of places. The elms of Brighton have become an increasingly distinctive feature of a town so far relatively unaffected by Dutch Elm Disease. London is famous for its magnificent planes; Derbyshire its ashwoods and Bournemouth its pines.

10. Grow trees to make places

An individual tree can create a place - with beauty, atmosphere and myriad cultural and historical associations. Groves of trees were endowed with spiritual significance by our Celtic forebears. Grow trees which will help to give meaning to a place - for people to congregate, places to muse, avenues to stroll along, landmarks and boundary markers. The uneasy presence of large trees in tubs, mobile and unrooted, emphasises the importance of growing trees to make places - not as ornaments to be moved around when they're in the way.

11. Welcome wildness

We should welcome wildness and discourage overtidiness. Ivy and wild clematis should be encouraged, deadwood should be left to add beauty and for wild life. After the southern storm in October, 1987, more viable trees died at the hand of man than were killed by the storm itself. A fallen tree is not a dead tree - with only a quarter of its roots left in the ground it may survive to produce many vertical stems. The shapes of trees tell stories of their lives - odd-shaped trees are fascinating characters, they excite our imaginations and are full of cultural and historical interest.

12. Design all new buildings around trees

Thousands of trees are ripped-up for new development each year. Many more are debilitated and die later due to soil compaction, by having roots severed and damage to trunk and branch by careless builders. By retaining existing trees when constructing new buildings, we can add maturity and richness as well as value to houses, offices, supermarkets, and carparks. Imaginative schemes for new development which take care of the trees already growing in an area must be encouraged. Care during the process of building should become second nature.

13. Don't axe garden trees

A mature tree brings shade, privacy and birdsong into your garden. Yet the first thing many people do when they move into a new home is cut down the trees - without a thought for the neighbours or previous owner. Don't always blame trees for structural damage - the reason could just as easily be clay or drought. Removing the tree may well aggravate the problem. Tell your neighbours how much you appreciate their trees. Care for your trees and they will enhance the aesthetic, wild life and monetary value of your property. Get them protected by law if you move on.

14. Find new uses for old woodland

In order to stop the destruction of deciduous woods we need to find new uses for small roundwood, expand our native hardwood industry and the market for wood products. We import the great majority of our timber needs - of all the wood used in Britain, 90% comes from other countries. Encourage good traditional practices of woodmanship, such as coppicing and pollarding, and search for new ones. Working woodlands are good to walk in too - seek rights to use and enjoy local woods.

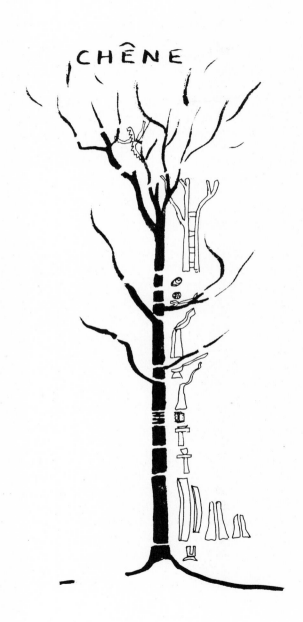

15. Save old orchards and fruit trees

Old orchards are disappearing fast. They are being grubbed-up and the land turned over to cereals, grass production and housing. New orchards with their rows of heavily pruned bushes bear no comparison to traditional orchards. 6000 varieties of apple are recorded in the National Apple Register of the UK, nowadays only 9 dominate in commercial orchards. Many places had their local varieties - reflected in names such as Cornish Gillyflower, Beauty of Bath and St. Edmunds Pippin. Grow more old, local varieties of fruit trees - and establish community, town and school orchards which can have many uses at the same time for birds, bees, fruiting, grazing, playing and peaceful relaxation.

16. Grow trees to help us breathe

Trees shield us from pollution. They improve the quality of the air we breathe, trapping dust particles and other pollutants and a big tree can provide a day's oxygen for up to four people. They are natural air conditioners, freshening and humidifying the air around them. Grow trees along busy roads, around towns, industrial areas and especially in car parks.

17. Make friends with a tree

Trees are not fragile ornaments, but tough, enduring, dependable creatures - if we treat them well. They are our friends and we can learn a tremendous amount from them. Get to know a tree from day to day, through the seasons, from decade to decade. Climb a tree, lean against it, feel its strength, stability and quietness. Trees have no voice - we must speak up for them.

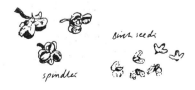

spindle

birch seeds

The destruction of the Tropical Rain Forests might seem a distant problem which is beyond our influence and unconnected with what happens in our own localities. It is not. Every tree is important. And unless we take more care of our own trees how can we honestly urge others to protect theirs? We can all make a difference by helping trees in our own places. This book is intended to encourage and inspire you to make a start.

In A Nutshell

Chapter 1 - **PRACTICAL CARE**

NATURAL REGENERATION

It is a fact of life that virtually all land, left unused, turns into woodland. At first it is what is disparagingly called 'scrub', in about 20 years the scrub begins to be recognised as 'woodland', and after another 30 years people imagine that it has always been oakwood. Anyone in a train can see different stages of the process on railway earthworks... To prevent trees from growing calls for constant effort. (Oliver Rackham, The Guardian, Jan. 1989)

Trees have been remarkably resilient to all sorts of changes. They have a natural ability to regenerate - if we let them they will come back. All trees want to grow - they will do all they can to succeed. We can help them a great deal by simply leaving them alone. Practical care for trees must begin with us stopping doing things which prevent trees from growing. We must create conditions which allow trees to flourish. An easy thing to do is to fence off an area of land to keep rabbits, deer and farm animals out, and simply sit back.

Trees came before us. They were flourishing in the Carboniferous period over 200 million years ago. As little as 2,000 years ago much of Britain was covered with huge tracts of wildwood. These primeval woods comprised a number of trees which invaded Britain from the south as the ice retreated from around 8000 B.C. onwards. The trees which crossed the land bridge between continental Europe and Britain before the sea level rose sufficiently to form a barrier to unaided migration, are known as our native or indigenous trees.

We carved ourselves out of this wildwood. Land has been cultivated and has reverted to woodland on numerous occasions. There are many woods on land once farmed which have not been planted by man but have regenerated naturally. Changes happen in a series of stages, the precise nature of which depend on soil conditions, climate, altitude and the availability of tree seed - as well as past use of the piece of land. The first tree invaders, or pioneers, of open land tend to be shrubs such as hawthorn and juniper, as well as birch. Elm and ash may then grow up gradually, outcompeting the earlier species for light and nutrients. These are then succeeded by the tallest trees: lime, beech and oak. Woodland is the stable and self-sustaining or climax vegetation - the natural garment - of most of Britain.

Most of our old established trees retain the ability to regenerate but modern changes (in geological terms) in climate and the introduction of other trees have had an effect. Due to climatic changes small-leaved lime appears to have lost its ability to seed naturally and non-native trees such as sycamore have proved very successful colonisers of woods and open gound. In order to start the process of change towards the natural climax woodland all we need to do is protect land from browsing animals and heavy use and natural regeneration will do the rest. Railway embankments, cuttings and many areas of unused open ground show evidence of this natural force and as far as possible should be left alone.

Probably none of the original woodland remains but there are many woods that have been with us for centuries. Woods that have existed for around 400 years are called ancient woodland and it is these areas which hold the richest historical, ecological and cultural interest. Find out about the ancient woodlands in your locality. The Nature Conservancy Council is compiling an inventory of ancient woodland on a county-by-county basis - contact your local office for more information. We must jealously guard these woodlands and ensure that no more are destroyed.

Further reading

The best books on trees and woods and the landscape of Britain are

Oliver Rackham, 1986, The History of the Countryside, J.M. Dent and Sons.
George Peterken, 1981, Woodland Conservation and Management, Chapman and Hall.
Hoskins, W.G., 1985, The Making of the English Landscape, Penguin

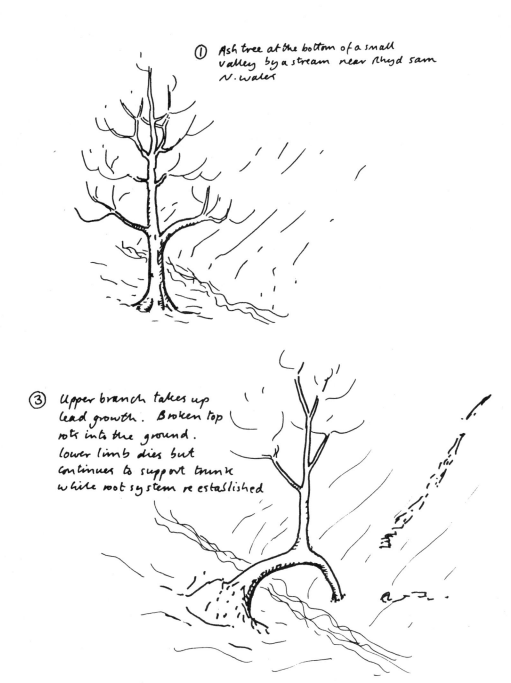

① Ash tree at the bottom of a small valley by a stream near Rhyd sam N. Wales

③ Upper branch takes up lead growth. Broken top rots into the ground. Lower limb dies but continues to support trunk while root system re established

② Tree blows over in a gale. Top breaks off.
Large limb supports remaining trunk,
forming an arch over the stream.

④ Lower limb rots off,
the tree continues its
upward growth

This "incident" in the life of
this tree had a duration of between
20 and 30 years

COPPICING AND POLLARDING

For thousands of years the regenerative capacities of our traditional woodland trees have been explored and exploited. Coppicing and pollarding have given timber of controlled dimensions, at the same time prolonging the life of the trees.

Coppicing, pollarding and hedgelaying are all perfectly adaptable to town gardens, roadsides and parks as well as woodland and field. It is better to coppice or pollard trees in new developments than to remove them. Old hedgelines should be kept and maintained by hedgelaying.

Coppicing involves the periodic cutting of a tree close to ground level. While the cut wood, or poles are put to various uses, the roots remain intact and the tree sends up new growth from the coppice stool. Most of our ancient woodland has been used in this way at some stage in the past and usually over a long period of time. The Neolithic Sweet Track across the Somerset Levels, made from thin poles of ash, hazel, elm, and oak laid together, provides evidence that coppicing was practiced more than 4,500 years ago.

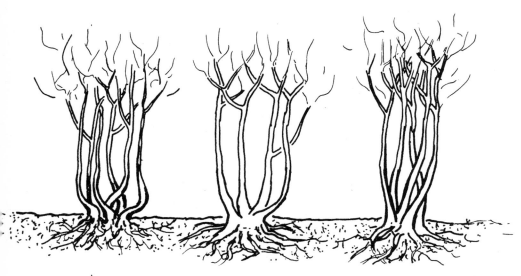

coppice .

David Mr '89

Commonly coppiced trees include sweet chestnut, hazel and hornbeam, although most native broadleaved trees will respond vigorously to this treatment. The period between cuts ranges from 15-25 years encouraging the tree to energetically throw up new shoots reaching12-15 feet in height. The cut or coppice wood was used for many purposes - fence poles, for building, or to make pulp for paper. Coppice woodland was often mixed with growth of timber trees in a system called coppice-with-standards. Standards are large trees, commonly oak, which were grown at a lower density and long rotation to provide timber for beams and frames of large buildings and ships. The standard trees were normally selected from saplings which had regenerated naturally and covered a wide age-range to ensure a regular supply of large wood. This system is an excellent way of locking-up carbon dioxide, one of the causes of global warming, as the standard trees are allowed to develop a full canopy, thus enabling them to take in more carbon dioxide than modern forest trees which are closely packed together.

Many of our favourite flowers are associated with woodland glades - bluebells, primrose, wood anenome. As woodland edge plants they flower best in lots of sunlight and thrive in coppiced woodland. Felsham Hall Wood in Suffolk enjoys a continuous record of coppicing stretching back more than 700 years. But in most places coppicing has declined dramatically and the carpets of flowers are being shaded out.

Pollarding is a similar practice where the tree is regularly cut at about 6-8 feet so that new shoots are above the height of grazing animals. Pollarded willows are common along ditches or rhynes in wet places as in the Somerset Levels, and around Cambridge. Other pollarded trees - hornbeam, oak and beech - can be found in many woods such as Epping Forest and the Forest of Dean. Wood pasture - the multiple use of land where pollarded trees are grown on land used for grazing - was a common practice on commonland and in deer parks. Regular pollarding of trees to reduce bulk and shade used to be a common practice in towns.

Traditional **hedgelaying**, a form of hedge maintenance, is also based on the regenerative capability of trees. Strong vertical stems, or pleachers, are partially cut a few inches above the ground and gently

Pollard Ash.   Davidson '89

bent over at an angle, from near horizontal to 45 degrees. New shoots head vertically for the light to form an impenetrable barrier. Hedgelaying is currently enjoying something of a revival as a better alternative to mechanical trimming.

All these practices are commonly carried out in the winter months, when the trees are not growing - new shoots being thrown out in the following spring. The roots remaining intact, the tree grows very quickly and its lifespan can be lengthened. In many rural areas there are people, often now retired, with a great deal of experience of caring for woodland and hedgerow. Do you know anyone who has this knowledge and these skills in your locality? Can you put their experience to good use?

CARING FOR OLD TREES

I fear those grey, old men of Moccas, those grey, gnarled, low-browed, knock-kneed, bowed, bent, huge, strange, long-armed, deformed, hunch-backed, misshapen oak men that stand waiting and watching century after century.

(Francis Kilvert, writing of the ancient wood pasture of Moccas Park, Herefordshire in 1876)

Old trees and woods are our best friends. They are a speciality of the British landscape. No other European country is so well furnished with trees of such antiquity. We should be proud of old trees and treat them with respect, as Kilvert implies. Minimum intervention in the growth of a tree should be your maxim. Trees have survived remarkably well for thousands of years without much assistance from us.

Yet we seem to want to exert our control, restrict their freedom and show them who's boss. We call them over-mature and senile and consider them dangerous. Many of the organisations and people dedicated to trees are the most prolific proponents of such preju-diced attitudes - being dominated by timber growing instincts.

An individual tree left alone will almost always outlive a human being. They don't have a natural lifespan like humans. Different types of tree however do have different life expectancies. Oak and yew are two of the longer lived trees - birch one of our shortest (but even a birch can live for well over 200 years). Many trees will take as long to decline as they do to grow. Dryden wrote,

The monarch oak, the Patriarch of the trees
Shoots rising up, and spreads by slow degrees
Three centuries he grows, and three he stays
Supreme in state, and in three more decays.

Old trees are full of character. Their unusual shapes and sizes inspire and excite. We should be more imaginative in our ideas of what a tree should look like. Trees when allowed to grow freely obey no aesthetic rules - that is part of their beauty and value. We need to confront our attitudes towards what is ugly and what is beautiful. The naturalist school of painting which grew in the last century reacted against the past tendency to idealise nature and the shapes of trees. It began to see beauty in all natural forms. Constable wrote,

The world is wide; no two days are alike, nor even two hours; neither were there ever two leaves of a tree alike since the creation of the world; and the genuine productions of art, like those of nature, are all distinct from each other.

Our attitudes towards the shape of trees often extend beyond purely aesthetic or ecological considerations and reflect the nature of a particular form of management. In the context of feudalistic land-use it has been said,

The upper classes seem to have regarded the pollards as unattractive because by the eighteenth century they were a paricular feature of common land. Unlike the new plantations they symbolised the traditional systems of communal control over the exploitation of land." (Williamson and Bellamy, 1987, Property and Landscape)

Old trees don't have to be huge and towering. Fat carbuncled pollards can be many centuries old, as can coppices which may only

staghead oak.

be a few inches high but have huge stools, many feet round. The ash stool in Felsham Hall Wood is 18 feet in diameter and at least 1000 years old (Rackham, 1976).

Dead branches on living trees are a normal part of a tree's development. Old oaks and chestnuts often carry a number of large, dead branches high in the canopy, earning the description stag-headed. But stag-headedness does not indicate a dying tree. It is a sort of self-pruning, a way of adapting to changing conditions such as drought, a lowering of the water table, physical damage or stress. Stag-headed trees can go on for centuries.

Hollow trees are common. We should not worry unduly to see a tree whose trunk is not completely intact. There is no reason why a hollow tree can't go on living for many years - and many do for centuries. Life-giving water and nutrients are transported in a layer called the cambium, between the inner edge of the bark and the dead wood.

In spite of being rotten inside, this tree was in fairly good condition. A tree is not useful to man, of course, for timber, if internally decayed either by disease or the tooth of time; but its own health is not affected if the outer sheaths of the trunk are all right, because the life of a tree resides in and receives reinforcement at its circumference and not its centre. (Collis, 1973, The Worm Forgives the Plough)

Old hollow and stag-headed trees are of great value for wild life - providing food for fungi and insects, places to nest and shelter for bats, owls and other birds. The oaks of Moccas Park themselves support almost 100 species of lichen and many insects, some particular to them alone. If old trees disappear then so do many of these plants and animals. The tendency to tidy things up goes against everything old trees and woods stand for. Dead wood provides a home for a host of plants and creatures, as well as ultimately enriching the woodland soil.

This Solitary Tree. A living thing
Produced too slowly ever to decay
of form and aspect too magnificent
to be destroyed.   William Wordsworth

GROWING FRUIT TREES

We have a rich inheritance of wild fruit trees - sloe, apple, elderberry, wild cherry, bullace, cherry plum, medlar, wild pear, juniper. These are the forbearers of our domestic fruits, good for wild life, beautiful in blossom, enriching our hedgerows and woodland diversity and their genetic variety provides a vital library to which we can keep on returning for ideas for new books! They are often treated as poor country cousins to the big timber trees - but their wood is much sought after for domestic uses. They are capable of long life (crab apples are often mentioned on old parish boundary maps), and some of our favourite fruits have appeared spontaneously as sports in the woods, such as the Victoria plum. In wood, hedgerow and garden we should encourage our wild fruits to flourish where they feel most at home.

It's exciting to grow fruit trees from pips. The resulting tree will never produce fruit exactly the same as its parent, but you may nurture a new variety which has its own qualities. The original Bramley apple tree is still growing in a cottage garden in Southwell, Nottinghamshire, crooked and leaning, over 170 years after the pip was planted. Every Bramley apple tree can be traced back, through grafts of grafts, to this single tree.

A fruit tree will bring blossom, birds and bees into your garden, as well as giving you the opportunity to pick your own fruit at its prime, free from pesticides and preservatives. If you're not too worried about an edible crop, any wild fruit tree will attract wild life.

To grow a specific variety of fruit tree you must learn to graft or bud. This involves taking small slices of carefully selected living wood from your chosen variety and joining this onto a pruned rootstock or large branch of another tree. It is an ancient practice and there are many ways to do it.

To **bud**, prune off a new shoot, about 6-12 inches long, in the summer. Buds are found at the point where leaf stalks branch off from a new shoot. After gently stripping the leaves from the shoot, carefully slice off a single bud with a sharp knife and insert it into a shallow cut or chip cut into the bark of the receiving tree.

Grafting involves taking scions or graftwood from new shoots. Scionwood is prepared by trimming shoots down to about 3-4 buds and cutting one end at an angle. Place the cut end into a cut or cleft made into rootstock which has been sawn across. Ensure that the cambium, or living part, of both scion and rootstock are in contact. Cut new shoots for grafting in January and stand in moist soil until early spring, when the grafting should be done.

New budding or grafting should be protected for a while with tape and grafting wax (ask at your local nursery). The bud or graft should grow between 2-3 feet in the following growing season.

Grafting is simpler than it sounds - it's harder to describe than to actually do it! Any good gardener or allotment holder should be able to show you how to graft. You can duplicate your own favourite variety in this way and ensure its survival. Exchange graftwood with your neighbours or take it from an old tree you know fruits well. You could grow varieties of fruit on existing hawthorn rootstock in a hedge. Try rootstock of other small trees or shrubs - many are compatible with fruit trees. If you don't have any, some nurseries can supply rootstock for this purpose. (Some may be willing to do the grafting for you)

If there aren't many different varieties in your neighbourhood and you're not confident about doing your own grafting you could visit a local nursery. There are many nurseries supplying a wide range of varieties of different kinds of tree fruit, including quince, medlar and cherry. Scotts Nurseries, Merriott, Somerset have a wide selection - write for a copy of their informative catalogue. If you can't get hold of bud or graftwood or otherwise obtain a particular variety, you could try the National Fruit Trials, at Brogdale, Faversham, in Kent or the Royal Horticultural Society Garden at Wisley who may be able to supply what you need from their own collections.

Most nurseries are able to supply trees on any one of a number of rootstocks - from those (called M27, M9, M26 and MM106) which produce various sizes of dwarf tree - as little as 3 feet tall - to standard rootstock producing large, traditional trees. Wherever possible try to plant a standard or half-standard tree. These have a longer lifespan - over 100 years in many cases and will also need less attention. Dwarfing trees, although bearing their first fruit in just 3-4 years - where standards take 8-10 years, will have much shorter lives, often less than 30 years. They will not produce as much fruit as a large tree but must be permanently staked as the weight of fruit might still be enough to destabilise the tree. They will also require careful pruning and only do well on fertile soils. Above all that they don't have the charm of taller trees.

Where space is limited you might choose to grow a fruit tree on dwarfing rootstock - but you must be prepared to give them the extra attention they require. You can fan-train trees against a sunny wall if that's all the space you have. A semi-dwarfing, MM106 rootstock, will be best for this.

Most fruit trees require another variety to assist pollination. Some, such as the apple Blenheim Orange, prefer two other varieties. To ensure a good crop you need to have trees quite close to each other, around 6-8 feet apart for standard or half standard trees, to encourage cross pollination. You should be careful to select varieties which will blossom at roughly the same time. To help you, fruit trees are grouped into pollination groups according to the time of blossom. Choose varieties in the same group for best results.

Don't write-off a fruit tree that has been damaged or blown-over by high winds. Along with other deciduous trees, they will often thrive leaning on their sides - and picking the fruit will be a lot easier. After the Great Storm of October, 1987, Cecelia Lazarus bravely hung on to her Bramley apple and William pear trees which had fallen but which still had roots in the ground. Her mother had planted them in her small, north London garden over 50 years before. Sure enough a profusion of blossom appeared in the spring and a respectable harvest followed. What's more she can now reach the fruit from the ground and sit on the reclining trunks amongst the blossom and bees.

You should also select wild fruits and domesticated varieties which will do well in your locality. A few varieties are able to grow in a range of places and quite difficult conditions. Bramley, Blenheim

In A Nutshell

Orange, Lord Derby and Wyken Pippin are amongst the hardiest apples. Others are quite choosy about soils they like and they may be particularly susceptible to frost. Many varieties of fruit have local associations, often reflected in their names such as Cornish Gilly-flower, St. Edmund's Russet, Cambridge Gage and Warwickshire Drooper. Select those which already grow or are known to have grown well in the past in your locality. George Morris, who has spent many years researching the apples of Yorkshire, lists some 25 different varieties of apples "either still growing or remembered as having grown during the early years of this century in Ryedale."

Further reading

Lawrence D. Hills, 1984, The Good Fruit Guide, Henry Doubleday Research Association
Harry Baker, 1986, The Fruit Garden Displayed, R.H.S.
Scott's Nurseries, Catalogue, Scotts of Merriott, Merriott, Somerset
Francesca Greenoak, 1983, Forgotten Fruit, Andre Deutsch
Geoffrey Grigson, 1975, The Englishman's Flora, Paladin
Rosanne Sanders, 1988, The English Apple, Phaidon
Virgil, (Trans. L.Wilkinson), 1982, The Georgics, Penguin
Save Our Orchards, free leaflet (on receipt of sae) from Common Ground, 45 Shelton Street, London WC2

PRUNING AND CARING FOR DAMAGED TREES

The tree which moves some to tears of joy is in the eyes of others only a green thing which stands in the way. Some see nature as all ridicule and deformity ...... and some scarce see nature at all. But by the eyes of a man of imagination, nature is imagination itself.

(William Blake, in a letter to Dr. Trusler)

Pruning should be carried out with restraint. Deadwood which is created as part of the natural growth process should be left until it falls naturally. Only for safety's sake or in the case of fruit trees, where the production of an annual crop of fruit is the goal, should pruning be carried out as a matter of course. The removal of branches may be necessary to prevent obstruction or damage to buildings. Pollarding, coppicing and hedgelaying are all forms of pruning.

Pruning is quite simple once a few basic principles are understood. The cut should always be made beyond a new shoot, which has been chosen to encourage the tree to grow in a particular direction. The cut should be angled to allow rainwater to drain-off easily. Pruning should be done whenever possible, in the winter months when the sap in broadleaf trees is not rising. (Try planting some of the smaller prunings, many types of tree will grow vigorously from cuttings).

A S H   D O M E

Most people prune trees to achieve a standard shape. Sculptor David Nash uses pruning as a means of creating beautiful works, often with evocative names, such as his ash dome, willow ladder, divided oaks and turning pines.

Pruning fruit trees to encourage a good crop is slightly more compli-
cated, and depends on the age of the tree. Generally main branches,
or leaders, are pruned back by up to a third with a young tree, to help
shape it. Pruning to encourage fruit production depends on type of
fruit and the fruit-bearing habit of the tree (see Harry Baker, 1986)

Trees that have been windblown or have fallen for some other
reason should not be assumed dead. Shortly after the Great Storm
of October, 1987, we rushed out the following messages on simply
produced postcards - 70,000 of them. Although the storm only
affected the south east, the message has a relevance and urgency
anywhere trees are damaged by wind or accident:

DON'T CHOP THEM DOWN   DON'T CHOP THEM UP

*The great storm of October 16th brought down many beautiful trees. But
a fallen tree is not a dead tree...with only a quarter of its roots left in the
ground, it may survive and become a fascinating old character. Even large
trees will grow horizontally given half the chance. Only if a tree has fallen
dangerously should removal be the sole option... otherwise wait and see.
Insects, birds and animals need old trees and so do we.*

*Remedial action may be necessary: careful pruning of broken roots and
branches, firm replacing of soil to ground level leaving no pockets of air
around the roots: some branches should be cut right back to decrease the
work of the reduced root system. Most broadleaf trees will fight to live and
at the very least attempt new growth from the uninjured roots growing
much more quickly than a newly planted tree: many will grow up vertically
from the crowns and trunk.*

*These trees will add character as well as beauty to our gardens, parks and
landscape, reminders of the great storm, old friends to play and muse upon.*

*It may be possible to carefully upright trees which are leaning immediately
or in stages over a few weeks (keep roots protected). Trees are remarkably
resilient, the roots having been 'naturally' pruned, and may grow vigorously to re-establish the tree or rapidly put up new growth from the base
next spring.*

In A Nutshell

Cut damaged and heavy branches for safety and stability. Heave back with help and care, dig the roots gently into the soil, tread down firmly, leaving no air pockets around the roots. Place stakes on the windward side to help anchor the tree (3 feet down and one third the tree's height) taking care of the roots, and secure with plastic tree ties.

For broadleaf trees which have been rocked or whose main branches have been badly damaged, consider pruning hard back or if necessary pollarding (cutting across the trunk at some height) or coppicing (cutting close to the ground). We have used trees in this way for centuries, they grow back very quickly because their root systems are well established; it can prolong their lives.

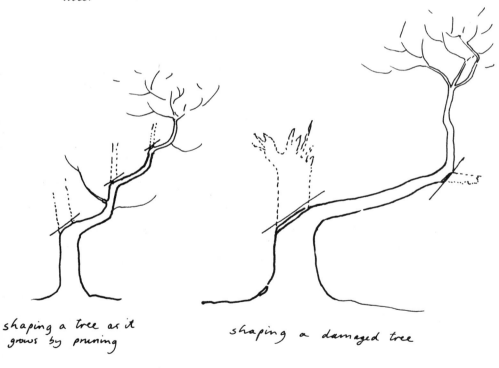

shaping a tree as it grows by pruning

shaping a damaged tree

With care you should be able to do most light pruning yourself. For jobs that you feel unsure about, which may involve climbing a tree or the removal of particularly heavy branches, it would be wise to seek advice from an approved tree contractor.

But remember:
- never accept the view of casual callers who may tell you that a tree is dangerous and requires cutting back or down.
- contact the council's tree officer for advice and if necessary a list of local contractors.
- a list of approved tree specialists throughout the country is kept by the Arboricultural Association.
- if you have a bad experience with a contractor, report it to your tree officer - otherwise half the trees in your neighbourhood might disappear.

Further reading

Alan Mitchell, 1981, A Gardener's Book of Trees, J.M. Dent and Sons
Countryside Commission, 1988, Task Force Trees - Action Pack
David Nash, 1983, Sixty Seasons, Third Eye Center
David Nash, 1987, Wood Primer, Bedford Press Books
Harry Baker, 1986, The Fruit Garden Displayed, R.H.S.

Fallen Ash

GROWING YOUR OWN TREES

We have an obsession for **planting** trees and then we forget about them. We seem to ignore the natural process of reproduction through their own seed. We can aid and speed this process in many ways. Collecting and growing tree seeds and growing trees from cuttings is an exciting thing to do - and is not difficult at all - squirrels and jays do it all the time. Tree seeds in the wild face myriad dangers - foraging animals, squirrels, mice, farmer's ploughs, grazing deer, walker's feet, herbicides are just some of them.

For 3 years he had been planting seeds in the wilderness. He had planted one hundred thousand. Of the hundred thousand, twenty thousand had sprouted. Of the twenty thousand he still expected to lose about half, to rodents or to the unpredictable designs of Providence. There remained ten thousand oak trees to grow where nothing had grown before. (Giono, 1985).

Others would suggest but 1 in 100,000 would struggle to treehood.

There are many good reasons for growing trees from seed collected locally;

- local trees are more likely to be adapted to local climate and soils;
- you can reinforce local distinctiveness;
- you will be conserving the local genetic stock;
- many nurseries and seed suppliers import their stock - even of native trees;
- and it's free.

The usual time to collect seeds is in the autumn, just before the leaves and fruit begin to fall. Fruit or berries which contain seeds should be collected when fully ripe but it is wise not to wait too long as such items are avidly gathered and eaten by birds, squirrels and other animals. Ivy berries won't be ready until early spring - a fact the birds appreciate! You can collect seeds whilst walking in gardens, parks and local woods. Most can be gathered from the ground or directly from the tree. Be sure that nuts do not have holes in them and are not empty or deformed.

Seed should be collected from healthy looking trees and preferably from trees growing close to other trees of the same type. Isolated individual trees should be avoided wherever possible as their seed may not germinate well due to self-pollination. Also avoid trees that are obviously diseased. Most trees over 20 years old yield a good quantity of seed - some, such as birch, may produce copious seed after only 10 years. Even oak with a reputation for slow growth can reach a height of over 20 feet in as many years and can be vigorously producing acorns.

Collected seed should be put in bags which allow them to breathe, such as a hessian sack or an old sock. They should be kept in cool, airy conditions. After collection they can be treated in different ways depending on the kind of seed. There are four main kinds -

- one or a number of seeds contained in berries or fruit which may occur in clusters or individually, such as hawthorn, rowan, apple, holly and ivy.
- nuts, often occuring in clusters and sometimes edible, such as walnut, hazel, oak, and beech.
- winged seed, the wings encouraging dispersal, for example ash, field maple, sycamore and hornbeam.
- and cones, which contain a number of seeds, for example Scot's pine and alder.

alder cones

Many tree seeds, particularly the nuts, can be sown immediately after collection in September or October, in open ground or in pots, allowing about 4 inches between each. For better results the seedbed could be dug over lightly and weeded. A well sheltered spot is best

- surrounded with good cat/rabbit/mouse proof wiremesh. Most of the nuts will germinate in the first spring after collection. Birch is one of the easiest of common trees to grow from seed. Other kinds of seed can be sown immediately in this way, such as hawthorn, field maple, hornbeam and holly, but will not normally germinate until the second spring after collection - in the case of holly you may have to wait even longer.

Seeds can be extracted from cones by slow drying in a warm room. The seeds can be collected in a tray as they drop out. Once collected these seeds can, like most winged seeds be kept in a dry, sealed container in cool conditions and sown in open ground or pots the following spring.

An alternative method of germinating seed, where there's limited space and you want more control over the process, involves stratification. This is a method of breaking a seed's natural period of dormancy. The seed is mixed with sand and put in a large pot or biscuit tin pierced with holes to ensure good drainage and airflow. Seeds contained in fruit or berries can be separated easily from the flesh by soaking in warm water beforehand. Keep moist in a cool, dark place. Seeds are ready to sow carefully into prepared open ground when swollen and a growing shoot or root appears.

Many trees will not grow true from seed. You can't grow a Black Worcester pear from a pip of that parentage or a Japanese maple just like your own. This needn't be a problem - it can be exciting to see how it turns out - many of our finest varieties of edible fruit have been the result of chance seedlings.

A number of common trees cannot be grown by seed as they either do not produce seeds or the seed cannot easily be made to germinate. Many of these will have originated in warmer climes and include gingko, the plane tree and small- leaved lime.

Some trees such as willow, elder, poplar and privet, can be easily grown from cuttings. You can grow willows simply by pushing 1 foot long willow stems in autumn, into a damp patch of ground. Leave about half of the cutting showing above ground. Not all will grow but if conditions are right many will sprout in spring.

A number of trees regenerate by throwing up new growth or **suckers** from the roots. Elm is famous for this. Many an elm badly ravaged by Dutch Elm Disease has thrown-up shoots after the trunk has been removed. I know of one ancient elm tree once a focal point of a village on the South Downs which had been accused of obstruction by new owners and cut down to a small stump around which new growth has sprung-up in profusion - much to the joy of local people sad at losing the tree. Cherry, lime, aspen and tree of heaven also produce suckers in this way. You can grow any of these trees by carefully taking out of suckers with their own small root systems.

Layering is a kind of induced suckering whereby shoots or stems close to the ground are gently bent (they can be partially cut if this helps) and buried, pegged down into the ground and covered with soil. Hazel, fig, dogwood and many other shrubs will respond to layering. Do it before Christmas while the soil is still warm. After about a year the stem will have developed its own roots and is ready to be cut and replanted.

Further Reading

Liebscher, K., 1978, Tree Nurseries, BTCV

Bolam, S., Phillips, J., and Yoxon, M., The Collection and Storage of Native Trees and Shrub Seeds, in Milton Keynes Development Corporation, 1977, Ecological Studies in Milton Keynes - 18 Creative Conservation Part 1

Ayres, A., (Ed), 1988, The Gardening From Which? Guide to Successful Propagation, Consumer's Association/Hodder and Stoughton

Avon County Council, Growing Trees from Acorns, leaflet

Jean Giono, 1985, The Man Who Planted Trees, Chelsea Green Publishing Co.

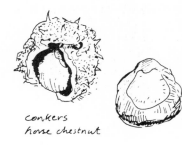

conkers
horse chestnut

PLANTING AND TRANSPLANTING

The holes were already dug, and they set to work. Winterbourne's fingers were endowed with a gentle conjurer's touch in spreading the roots of each little tree, resulting in a sort of caress under which the delicate fibres all laid themselves out in the proper directions for growth. He put most of these roots towards the south-west; for, he said, in forty years' time, when some great gale is blowing from that quarter, the trees will require the strongest holdfast on that side to stand against it and not fall.

(from Thomas Hardy, the Woodlanders, 1888)

Wherever possible you should try to sow and germinate seed in the place you want the tree to eventually grow. As well as reducing labour this will increase the tree's chances of survival. Tree planting, or rather transplanting, is an unnatural process. It must be done with the utmost care. As Rackham puts it "a planted tree is an injured tree: even a one year-old oakling has an enormous root-system that is injured by being dug-up from the ground or restricted by being grown in a pot." It is uprooted from the soil it has grown to know and love, the balance between the roots and leaves is disturbed, it is stored in unnatural conditions and then put back in the ground in a place with which it is entirely unfamiliar. This is a disturbing enough process for humans let alone a plant - which has not evolved with mobility in mind. You only need transplant when growing seed in a tree nursery or in pots on a balcony and when thinning out seedlings. Also when seeds or cuttings are not available locally and a more immediate impact is required, then planting with a young tree will be the only option.

When to plant

With broadleaved trees planting is best done in the late autumn and winter, preferably before the ground gets hardened with frost - a good rule is to plant before Christmas. It is possible to plant trees right up to March or until new growth begins in the spring. If roots are left undisturbed seedlings grown in pots can be planted out at any time of the year with care. Because the leaves of evergreen trees are working throughout winter, they should be planted in early Spring when the roots begin to grow again.

What to plant

There aren't many places in which some kind of tree will not grow - as long as basic requirements are met - adequate soil, a reasonable amount of light, plenty of moisture and not too polluted air. Most types of tree have their favourite places.

Sycamore and ash do well in coastal situations despite the salt spray and provide valuable shelter in many places. Holm, or evergreen, oak also does particularly well in these conditions - providing all year round shelter. Some trees are able to cope with polluted city air. The London Plane is perhaps the best known example - helped by shedding its bark in the early autumn. In the north native black poplar, or Manchester Poplar, does well in towns. Some trees don't like soils which are either too chalky or too acid. Beech does well on both. Rowan, birch and Scots pine all do well on heathy, acid soils, associated with heather and bracken. Oaks and hornbeam like wet, heavy clay soils best.

Many non-native trees - horse chestnut, London plane, weeping willow - make a big contribution to the character of our towns and cities.

london plane

Different types of tree carry with them different cultural associations. Be alert to the meaning of particular trees. If we do not respect these associations we will only diminish their value. In the country choose a suitable tree by looking at what's already growing naturally around you, in local woods, fields and hedges. Don't plant a tree just because it's cheap or easy to obtain.

Where to plant

When trees are planted or pruned without regard for the special places they create, they are as good as dead for the people who need them.

(Alexander et al, 1977, A Pattern Language).

Trees make places - real places to meet, play in, relax and simply enjoy. The tree in the village square has been so important for local culture for many centuries. A single tree can put identity into a place. It's removal can be devastating.

When planting trees be wary of treating them as merely inanimate ornaments in the landscape, to be moved around at will. Do not relegate trees to odd corners or left-over spaces. The current vogue for large trees-in-tubs disturbs our deep knowledge of the rootedness and longevity of trees, they only seem to be half there - sad for the tree and sad for the place. Nevertheless some greenery in a sterile place is welcomed and will do a valuable job improving the air. Small trees in half-barrels - like bay or laurel may also bring us a breath of other countries.

'Trees in Tubs' by Kathleen Raine

Little laurel trees, your roots can find
No mountain, yet your leaves extend
Beyond your own world, into mine
Perennial wands, unfolding in my thought
The budding evergreen of time.

Beware of planting in areas of archaeological and historical importance - tree roots disturb old bones.

How to plant

How to plant will depend very much on the age of the tree and where it is going to be planted. Generally the smaller the tree the easier the job.

If you have to move seedling trees that you have grown yourself it is best done 2-3 years after germination. This should allow the seedling sufficient time to have established itself and will reduce damage to roots in moving - but take care, a small pot can restrict root growth after only one year. Also it will not require a supporting stake. All you need to do is dig a small hole but big enough to accommodate the roots comfortably and loosen the surrounding soil - this will help the roots to anchor. The soil could be enriched by compost, preferably organic, leaf mulch, to help it retain water. The soil should be replaced carefully around roots, pressing firmly to avoid creating air pockets, which will cause the roots to dry out and die. A good soaking with water will help close any air pockets.

When buying a larger tree from a nursery always make sure it has a strong and healthy looking main stem or leading shoot. These trees will have been either container grown or at some stage dug-up out of open ground. In the former case the roots will most likely be constricted in a root ball and should be gently spread out as far as possible without breaking them. This will make it easier for the roots to anchor themselves quickly.

A large tree is also likely to require secure staking. A stake about 8 feet high should be driven down about 3 feet into the soil before the tree is put in position, to avoid damage to roots, ideally on the windward side roughly 1 foot from the final position of the main stem. Recent research suggests it might be better to use a smaller stake which reaches about a third of the way up the stem and allows the top to sway in the wind increasing the strength of the stem.

The main stem should be attached to the stake with plastic/rubber ties in at least two places - 1/3 and 2/3 of the way up the stem. Ties should be securely fixed to the stake. They should be regularly checked and loosened to make sure the stem isn't being strangled as it grows. Remove the stake once the tree has established itself, usually after 2 to 3 years. Check to see if it is safe by gently rocking the tree - if it doesn't return to the upright position it's not ready. Prompt removal of the stake will encourage roots to tighten their grip in the soil and protect against high winds. Younger whips, around 3-4 feet high will usually not need a stake, their roots will react vigorously to waving by the wind.

A planted tree needs plenty of water. In Spring even a small tree can drink up to 2 gallons of water each day. A bucket every day during the dry summer months will be a great help. A large amount of water all at once is better as it should drain deep into the soil and feed the roots rather than surface vegetation. For the first few years careful hoeing and removal of competing plants a few feet around the tree will reduce water demand.

Don't automatically assume that planting an older and larger tree will have a greater impact in a shorter time. Older trees when planted are likely to suffer more from growth retardation due to stresses experienced during planting and being pot-bound. Inevitable damage to roots when planting will have an immediate impact above ground level. In its new surroundings the tree is likely to require more resources to cope with loss of shelter and in simply adapting to a new environment. This places more demands on the weakened root system which again checks tree growth. A younger 2-3 year old seedling or a whip (one or two years older) is likely to get off to a better start.

Tree protection

Whether you decide to protect a planted or grown tree will depend very much on where the tree is, its size and cost implications. In gardens there is usually no need to protect against large grazing animals, but some kind of protection may be needed against rabbits, squirrels, deer or dogs and accidental knocks by a lawn mower or bouncy children.

Protection available for individual trees ranges from iron/metal guards to plastic spiral and tube guards. The former will be strong and effective against grazing by large animals, cattle and deer and will hopefully last a long time. But they will be costly, so make sure you choose one that is high enough and wide enough for many years protection. Spiral guards wound around the stem of a small tree will protect against rabbit nibbling. Plastic tubing, 2-3 feet high, not only protects trees from grazing rabbits and deer, it also creates warm, moist conditions, conducive to rapid growth. Tubes are conspicuous however and not very attractive. They will themselves need staking and although they will break up they do not entirely disintegrate after their useful life of around 5 years. (Beech doesn't do well in plastic tubes, appearing not to like the humid conditions).

When planting a small group of trees, to make a copse or woodland, the cost of individual tree protection will be quite high and might be prohibitive. Aesthetic considerations might rule out the use of individual protection in this case. An alternative would be to ensure the area of trees is securely fenced-off to protect from large grazing animals such as sheep, deer and cows as well as rabbits and mice. Strong wooden stakes with fine mesh wire netting buried a few inches in the soil should be appropriate.

If you want to establish a small area of trees using seedlings or whips, plant individuals about 5-6 feet apart to allow enough room for undisturbed growth. You could try planting trees closer together so that they grow into each other and create interesting shapes. Avoid planting in regimented rows, especially close to the edge of the area, where you might consider planting smaller trees such as hazel, dogwood, holly or spindle.

There will be occasions when it's better to plant a mixture of trees. This will add diversity and interest to the wood, make it look more natural and will aid tree establishment. Nurse crops are often used in commercial woodlands to encourage faster growth. Oak nursed by larch can grow up to 25% faster than if planted alone. Growing a mixture of trees will provide more protection from high winds, be visually more attractive and can reduce the risk of disease. Disease of beech is less likely when grown with pine. The Forestry Commission suggest growing ash with alder or sycamore; beech with cherry; and oak with alder, ash, cherry or sweet chestnut. If you're planting a small copse on a hill-top it might be best to plant just one type of tree, such as beech. Always consider what grows best and is appropriate locally - if you don't follow local experience, make sure you have good reasons.

Further Reading

Countryside Conservation Handbook, 1979, Leaflet 3 The Planting and After-care of trees and shrubs, Countryside Commission
Tree Council, Why Pay Twice for a Tree? and Tree Planting and Maintenance (both leaflets)
Alan Mitchell, 1981, A Gardener's Book of Trees, J.M. Dent and Sons
Brooks, A., 1980, Woodlands - A Practical Conservation Handbook, BTCV

Contact the tree officer in the district or county council for details of any practical leaflets they might produce.

Chapter 2 - **WHAT YOU CAN DO**

IN YOUR GARDEN, PATIO OR BALCONY.

If you want to lay out a garden in front of your house and on the very spot there was a tree that's stood there for centuries, however old and gnarled you would not cut it down to make room for flower beds. You would plant your flower beds round the old tree. You could not grow a tree like that in a year

(Tolstoy, in Anna Karenina)

The Benefits of Garden Trees

Garden trees are a continual source of pleasure, contributing to the character and beauty of our surroundings - they can:

- provide seasonal variation with blossom, summer shade and autumn colours
- improve the air, releasing oxygen, absorbing carbon dioxide, removing dust and humidifying the atmosphere
- attract and sustain birds, butterflies and other wild life, including tree-loving plants such as ivy and mistletoe
- bring interest and variation to your garden
- provide home grown fresh fruit
- add to the value of your house
- increase privacy
- provide free play-frames for children
- and deaden noise.

Make your garden into an oasis of wildness and peace, places where trees and wild life can flourish.

Tree Care

It is important to care for the trees that you have. Generally they will grow happily, once well established, without our intervention, but there may be instances when they need some attention for example when growing close to buildings or after particularly high winds.

Some trees can be kept to a manageable size by careful pruning, coppicing and pollarding.

Which Sort of Tree?

The trees that will do best in your garden are likely to be those that are commonly found in the surrounding countryside or town. They will be best suited to local soils and climate. By planting them you'll be enhancing the distinctive character of where you live. You don't have to have a large garden to grow trees. Many, such as birch, rowan, hawthorn and elder, will be particularly suited to small gardens. They don't grow very big and cast little shade - if they grow too tall you can coppice or pollard them.

coppice.

A birch tree can be beautiful in a garden - they are graceful and fast growing and birds such as blue tits and great tits will feed off the insects they attract. Yew, holly and ivy will provide the birds with winter roosting and food.

Fruit trees can be successfully grown against walls which get a lot of light - trained in fans or as espaliers. You can see wonderful examples of fruit trees for small gardens at the Royal Horticultural Society Gardens, at Wisley, Surrey and in many old stately home kitchen gardens. Share the produce of your garden fruit trees with the birds - they'll eat the aphids on your roses and the leather jackets in your lawn.

Hedgerows

Plant a hedge to mark a boundary of your garden typical of the ones in your locality which may be a mixture of fast-growing hawthorn and field maple, with some holly and yew, or just one type of tree such as beech - they make beautiful garden hedges and are good for wild life. Privet hedges will also attract birds, butterflies, and insects - if allowed to flower. With beech, a trim in the late summer will help the leaves to stay on the branches thoughout the winter.

Grant Aid

You might be able to obtain some financial assistance for planting a tree, particularly in a position where it will be appreciated by many people, such as a front garden. In Dorset, Poole Borough Council run a project called 'Tree Scene' where, at the request of a house-holder, the council will plant a selected tree in their front garden. Other councils have schemes to support tree planting - ask your local tree officer for details of any grant aid that might be available.

Tree Protection

You should protect your garden trees with a Tree Preservation Order. Ask your council tree officer to do this to ensure the tree is protected once you move on. Alternatively you might consider using a restrictive covenant in the deeds, preventing future owners from removing trees you value. Ask your solicitor for help.

Trees on your patio or balcony

Even on the smallest balcony you can grow a wide variety of trees and create a beautiful space to gaze out on or to sit and relax in. The trees will attract wild life, birds and perhaps butterflies and bees - if it's not too high up.

In our own offices, near Covent Garden in Central London our two balconies, not much larger than 1 square yard support 10 different kinds of tree growing in pots. These are quite young and most have been grown from seed - including 2-year old oak seedlings and a horse chestnut. A hornbeam seedling was rescued from some grubby steps. A rowan, or Mountain Ash sucker, growing in a 10 inch pot has attained the grand height of more than 6 feet in just a few years. Blackbirds, sparrows, blue tits and greenfinches use the tree to perch on whilst queueing to feed. As soon as the trees grow too big they can be transplanted into a suitable place in your neighbourhood.

Fruit trees

A number of types of fruit tree, including apple, pear and even peach, can do well on small balconies in pots or trained-up walls. As well as providing a beautiful show at blossom time you will be able to pick your own pesticide-free fruit and eat it in its prime. A wall which receives plenty of sun will allow the fruit to ripen well and provide protection from cold winds. A Morello cherry tree, good for cooking and jam, will even do well on a north-facing wall. Branches should be carefully secured to strong canes attached to the wall at regular intervals - say every 3-4 feet. If you don't have a wall available you can grow dwarf trees in tubs as pyramids. A newly planted dwarf apple, on M26 dwarfing rootstock, will provide fruit within 3-4 years.

Good apple varieties for growing on your balcony include - Lady Sudeley, Egremont Russett, and King of the Pippins. Take care to plant appropriate pollinators. You can aid pollination yourself by brushing the blooms lightly with a soft paintbrush - or your cat's tail! (with cat still attached!) - in springtime to transfer the pollen.

Tree Care

Water copiously when growing trees in tubs as the roots have a limited area of soil in which to forage for moisture (unlike ground-rooted trees) but make sure the tubs or pots drain well. A good daily soak throughout the summer, and regular spraying of the foliage with water, and a diluted liquid manure, for example comfrey leaves or nettles soaked in water, once a week should help you produce a good crop. A regular leaf mulch collected from a local park or wood (seek permission first) will improve moisture content of soil. You could also cover soil with cold ashes, straw or even plastic to reduce moisture loss due to evaporation. Little watering will be necessary during the winter months.

Further reading

Alan Mitchell and John Jobling, 1984, Decorative Trees for Country, Town and Garden, HMSO
Arboricultural Association Leaflet, Trees for Small Gardens
Alan Mitchell, 1981, A Gardener's Book of Trees, JM Dent & Sons.
Kenneth and Gillian Beckett, 1979, Planting Nature Trees and Shrubs, Jarrold Colour Publishers.
Harry Baker, 1986, The Fruit Garden Displayed, Royal Horticultural Society
Keith Mossman, 1977, The Pip Book, Penguin
Robert Hart, 1988, The Forest Garden, The Institute For Social Inventions.

IN YOUR STREET

The elms are now at the height of their change. As I look down our street, which is lined with them, now clothed in their very rich brownish-yellow dress, they remind me of yellowing sheaths of grain....The street is a great harvest-home. It would be worth the while to set out these trees, if only for their autumnal value. Think of these great yellow canopies or parasols held over our heads and houses by the mile together, making the village all one and compact, an ulmarium. And then how gently and unobserved they drop their burdens and let in the sun when it is wanted, their leaves not heard when they fall on our roofs and in our streets.

(Thoreau, 1857, from 'The Heart of Thoreau's Journals', ed. O.Shepard)

Street trees have a big effect on the character of our towns. Tree-lined streets are associated with healthy and wealthy localities. Trees have been planted by councils for many years for the benefit of public health as purifiers of city air - trapping pollutants such as lead and dust particles, reducing noise and giving us oxygen. Street names such as Elm Grove and Walnut Tree Walk reflect the local importance of trees, which in some cases may have been present before the houses were built.

But street trees live in a hostile environment. Not only must they tolerate high levels of direct pollution from car exhausts but they are also susceptible to salt-sprays used to de-ice roads in winter, herbicides used in weed control, damage to roots during road repairs, not to mention being at risk from collisions with cars, excessive dogs and also vandalism. If you see a tree being damaged by a vehicle or vandal report it to the council tree officer immediately. People who damage trees wantonly should be prosecuted and fined.

Care of Street Trees

Street trees, especially when newly planted, need a lot of attention. Around one half of newly planted trees in urban areas die within 10 years. The majority die as a result of lack of water and nutrients, or because they have been badly planted, and not due to vandalism as is widely believed.
It is important to:
- water trees in your street regularly, especially during dry summer months,
- for the first few years after planting keep the ground around the tree free from competing plants by hoeing (best done in spring), add a leaf or straw mulch to control unwanted plant growth and help the soil hold moisture
- secure loose stakes and replace broken ties if necessary - free the tree if it is being strangled by a tie which is too tight
- ensure trees are not damaged by stacking building materials against the trunk, or during road and pavement repairs (wherever possible no excavations should take place under the canopy of the tree)
- quickly report any major damage, for example large broken branches, snapped stakes or broken tree ties, to the council - you could save a tree's life.

In A Nutshell

Responsibility for Street Trees

Many street trees are owned and looked after by the council and their care is usually the responsibility of an arboricultural officer in the council's works or parks/recreation department (sometimes the road and civil engineers department). They are usually not covered by Tree Preservation Orders.

A tree officer attached to the planning department is usually responsible for tree protection. In designated Conservation Areas the council must give 6 weeks notice to affected residents of any proposed work on street trees. This may include thinning or lopping branches or even complete removal. Proposed work is commonly contained on a register which you should be able to consult in the Council's planning department, and which may be circulated to local amenity groups. Ask the tree officer to do this if they don't already. If you don't like what is proposed you are entitled to object.

Outside designated Conservation Areas councils will sometimes inform residents before pruning, lopping or cutting down street trees - encourage them to keep you informed at all times. In an emergency contact the tree officer and ask why the work is being carried out - demand clear reasons. If you aren't satisfied let your local councillor, and even your MP, know what's happening and ask them to follow it up with those responsible as soon as possible. Rally support from neighbours. A letter in the local paper will often lend weight to your cause and may bring further support.

The trees have been there 70 years. People have come and gone in that time, but the trees have remained and I strongly feel they should remain an integral feature of Gladys Road. In fact some of the people who want the removal of these trees are moving out of Gladys Road - one is moving to a tree-lined road in Hall Green!
The tree which stands between my neighbour's house and our own has been earmarked for the chop! Neither of us want the tree to go. We feel no one has the right to take away a healthy tree from our home... I will do everything I can to stop them cutting down the tree outside our house. I will not accept its removal lying down. I am fighting the tree war in Gladys Road.

(excerpt from a letter to Birmingham Daily News, 1987)

New Street Trees

Ask the tree or arboricultural officer if you can have trees planted in your street if you don't already have some. Never accept the argument that because you are living in a town or city it might not be possible due to underground services, drainage and sewers, without questioning - this is often lazy, old fashioned thinking. Find out if your council has a tree sponsorship scheme whereby you could contribute to the cost of planting a tree outside your house. Agree with them a suitable location and an appropriate tree.

Further reading

Brian Clouston and Kathy Stansfield, (eds), 1981, Trees in Towns, Architectural Press

IN YOUR PARISH OR NEIGHBOURHOOD

What you have

It is important to value and hold on to the trees that you already have. Try to recall the trees and woods you know in your locality - where they are, what type, how they came to be there - you're likely to be surprised at how many there are. There will be many trees that you pass everyday - on the way to work or the shops - which you would greatly miss if they weren't there. Often people don't know that a tree is valued by others. Start by telling your neighbour how much you appreciate the trees in their garden.

You could start on a parish tree map of your locality. Show what trees are important to you in your neighbourhood, where and why - for climbing, bees, beauty. You could go on to gauge their age and condition and who's responsible for them. If a wood looks unused find out if there are any plans for it. It could be left alone, a wild, exciting, tanglewood, as a positive measure or new uses could perhaps be found for it.

Tree Protection

Check that as many trees as possible are protected by Tree Preservation Orders, (TPO's) or by some other form of legal protection. Consult the TPO records and map at the council planning office. Insist to the council's tree officer that Orders be placed on every tree in the neighbourhood. Groups of trees together could be protected by a single TPO. Some councils will only use a TPO if they consider a tree is under threat - tell the tree officer why you think a tree deserves to be protected. It is the tree officer's job to liaise with people and of course to care for trees.

A Tree Preservation Order is however, no guarantee of a tree's safety. It is always important to be vigilant. Keep a look out for any tell-tale signs, white crosses on trees, building work too close for comfort. If you see people working on trees in the neighbourhood ask them who has authorised the work and whether they have obtained permission to do it. Follow this up immediately by checking with the owners and council - let your feelings be known. If you think the work is being carried out illegally contact the council tree officer straight away, they can often move quickly to prevent a tree or wood being felled. You could call the police if you believe the law is being broken, sometimes simply the possibility of police involvement is enough to deter people. If this fails contact the local press and radio - encourage them to record the damage in some way, take photos, and pinpoint who's responsible. A local outcry might save a tree's life. It will help to set up a tree group so that a number of people can keep an eye out for changes.

More Trees

When you have done all you can to ensure the safety of existing trees in your parish you can think about how more trees can be grown.

To allow and encourage regeneration will always be the most effective and cheapest way to increase the number of trees in your parish. Planted trees need a lot of care and attention. Because their roots have been disturbed they will rarely do as well as seedling trees, which are allowed to germinate and flourish where they fall. Look for places in your locality which could be left alone for woodland to develop and wild life to enjoy - quiet corners in local parks, edges and corners of fields, roadside verges, unused allotments, woodland borders and railway embankments. You might also consider setting-up a parish tree nursery.

Hedgerows

Hedgerows are a potential linear wood. Different woody plants in hedges could be allowed to develop into beautiful trees with full canopies - and therefore absorbing more carbon. They already have established root systems and will develop rapidly requiring little maintenance. Hedgerow trees were a distinctive feature of much of our lowland landscape yet they are disappearing faster than the hedges themselves. Make sure all your local hedgerow trees are covered by a TPO.

With the farmer you can identify suitable saplings in hedgerows by marking or tagging. This is best done in the summer when tree identification is easier and before the hedges are trimmed. The purpose is to identify the tree so that the hedge-trimmers can avoid them. Use brightly coloured strips of strong plastic (cut up feed bags). Some County Councils supply specially made tree-tags free of charge for this purpose. By tagging carefully selected saplings you can add to the variety of hedgerow trees in your area, and don't forget wild fruit trees, cherry and bullace, they will be an added attraction to the birds.

Laying a hawthorn hedge.

The older the hedge the greater number of different trees you will have to choose from. Ash, oak, field maple, wild cherry, crab apple and holly can all be found growing in hedgerows. For a rough estimate of the age of a hedge count the number of species of tree or shrub in a 30 yard stretch - this will give the approximate age in centuries. Many hedges contain 4 or less different trees and date from the eighteenth or nineteenth century enclosure period - but 10 species really could mean the hedge is over 1000 years old.

Encourage hedgerow and tree retention in new industrial and housing developments - they provide instant beauty, maintain wild life and are a hint of past uses and cultural activities, such as hedgelaying. Look for old hedgerow trees in parts of town - take special care of them.

Further reading

Pollard, M.D. Hooper and N.W. Moore, 1974, Hedges, Collins
Richard and Nina Muir, 1987, Hedgerows- their history and Wild-life, Michael Joseph
Dowdeswell, W.H.,1987, Hedgerows and Verges Allen & Unwin
Countryside Commission Countryside Conservation Leaflet 9 - Tree Tagging
Tindall, G.,1977, The Fields Beneath, Granada

WHAT YOU CAN DO - IN YOUR SCHOOL

'Plant A Rowan In The School Yard' by Heather Harrison

The children gathered round,
two drew straws to dig the hole
and two to be allowed to hold the tree
and two to plant with spades and earth
and two to stamp the soil.
They all shared the planting,
a rite they marked with songs
with accounts recorded and read out
before the Whole School.

The unititiate were not impressed.
A three foot twig seems hardly worth the ceremony.

*Then, in the spring this year, to everyone's surprise
it flowered!
Such a spindle, trunk and limb.
Yet, ending each thin bough
bursts out a shag of bloom -
fat, cream, powder puffs of bloom!*

*"Do not pull that tree!" the teacher shouts.
How can they not?
The children run
to cup the blossom in their hands
to sniff the pollen dust
to pluck one tiny petal-head
to throw and see what "flutter" means
for it is their tree and
the only one at their head height.*

*The rowan has already served its purpose
bringing joy; and if it lives, well,
fruits will come.*

School grounds provide many excellent opportunities for trees which could improve and enrich the school surroundings, as well as providing a valuable resource for continuing study on the doorstep. School playing fields and playgrounds are all too often plain, flat and treeless expanses of grass or tarmac. This needn't be so. Much can be done to add variety and interest, whilst keeping areas open for communal activities and organised games.

A look at the boundaries might immediately suggest possibilities. Why not replace hard, unattractive fencing with hedges to soften the appearance and attract wild life? Tennis and netball courts could be sheltered effectively from winds by establishing a thick, evergreen hedge of holly and ivy and yew for all year round protection - as at Wimbledon! If you already have trees in the school grounds, ensure they are well cared-for, especially young, planted trees - water regularly during the summer; loosen ties - you could record a trees growth over a number of years. One Australian school links groups of children with particular trees in the yard and playing fields - these children lunch, sit and talk there - their affinity is always remembered.

Fruit Trees

Individual or small groups of trees can be planted in tarmaced areas if space is very limited. Espalier and cordon fruit trees can be trained-up walls and fencing. Why not consider planting apple or pear trees in the open? (If they are ever blown over they will often happily carry on growing and fruiting - as well as providing wonderful climbing frames and seats.)

Encourage children to plant the pips from the fruit they eat - in this way they will be able to watch their tree grow with them. The fruit will not be exactly the same as the parent - but there's a small chance it might taste just as nice! You might discover a wonderful new variety - the Grange Hill Pippin! If space permits consider establishing a small orchard. This needn't be a conventional orchard - it might be in a linear form along a boundary. You could keep bees as well to help pollination and supply the school with its own honey. Malorees School in North London has its own school orchard - with bees - which is cared for and used by the children and parent-staff organisation.

In A Nutshell

Tree Nursery

Set up a school tree nursery - where children can grow trees from collected seed and then give away saplings to people in the locality. The Scottish Community Woods Campaign organise Growing Up With Trees, a primary school tree nursery project,

Children usually get involved in Growing Up With Trees when they reach Primary 4, wherever possible collecting their own seed, always from Scottish native trees and shrubs. A small nursery is established in the school grounds (trees can be grown in pots if no ground is available) with the children looking after their trees until they reach Primary 7, when planting out can take place in the school grounds, at home or in local woods.

(Alan Drewer, Scottish Community Woods Campaign, 1988)

New Woods

If there is an unused or derelict part of the school grounds ask the Education Authority (usually the county or borough council) if the school-children, parents and staff - could work with the tree officer or a landscape architect to create a new woodland area. Discuss your ideas with the grounds maintenance staff, encourage them to become involved to help to ensure continued care for the newly created area. A parent/staff group will be able to help organise the project. Grant aid may be available from the county council and NCC - for fencing and cost of tools. You might even attract sponsorship from local companies. Advice and assistance could be sought from local nature conservation trusts. (See chapter 7 for more on sources of grant and advice.)

Children from many different cultural backgrounds at Walnut Tree Walk School in south London, worked with a landscape architect in 1987/8 to create a Far Eastern garden. With the help of a small grant from the borough council, they planted trees and shrubs from India, China and other parts of Asia - including Japanese maple, magnolia and gingko - in a small unused area of land in their playground.

Trees for People (141 London Road, St. Albans, Herts. AL1 1TA) run an annual national arboretum competition, with prizes up to £1000, for schools and youth groups with imaginative ideas for growing groups of trees.

Education and Promotion

You don't have to have trees in the school to learn about them - but it helps - even the names and sayings associated with trees - snottygogs will provoke interest! A school wood or orchard has enormous scope for educational activities across the curriculum for literature and art projects, as a subject of biology and science classes, you could even use woodland products - fruit and small timber in cooking and woodwork classes. Common Ground's book **Trees Be Company** is full of poetry about trees useful for secondary cross curricular use.

If you don't have space within the school grounds you could adopt a wood in the neighbourhood or trees in a nearby street, establish links with a farmer, wild life group or the Woodland Trust. Let other schools know what you are doing through the education authority and local press and radio. Invite journalists and photographers along to events such as planting and harvesting. You could be an inspiration to others.

Further reading

Chris Baines, 1985 How to Make a Wildife Garden, Elm Tree Books
Learning Through Landscapes Project - Technology House, Victoria Road, Winchester S)23 7DV (Eileen Adams)
Council for Environmental Education (School of Education, Reading University, London Road, Reading, RG12 5AQ) - plays a coordinating role for organisations involved in environmental education and produce a range of resource sheets and a monthly newsletter.
Heather Harrison, 1988, Roots Beneath the Pavement, West Midlands Arts/Common Ground
Green Teacher magazine - a monthly
Angela King and Sue Clifford, 1989, Trees Be Company, Bristol Classical Press (for Common Ground)
Scottish Community Woods Campaign - for more information on the Growing Up With Trees project.

In A Nutshell

IN YOUR WORKPLACE

You can help save trees simply by being careful about your use of products derived from them at work and at home. Each of us in Britain consumes on average two trees' worth of paper each year - over 100 million trees. It doesn't all have to made from virgin pulp. Our offices and kitchens are full of tropical hardwood. In 1984 we imported 1.5 million doors from tropical countries. You can help save the tropical rainforests by ensuring that you use timber which comes from tropical woods that are managed on a sustainable basis. Obtain a copy of the 'Good Wood Guide' from Friends of the Earth.

Paper re-use

You can immediately begin to reduce your own consumption of paper by making notepads for telephone messages from paper already used on one side; and by opening envelopes carefully and re-using them, where necessary with re-use labels. At Common Ground we have designed and had printed our own personalised re-use labels which we use and sell to others. You can do the same for your own organisation. By using your own re-use labels you not only show that you care for trees - they are also a good form of self-promotion.

Paper recycling

If your office or company has a particularly large consumption of paper you should contact a local waste paper merchant to see if they will pay for and collect waste paper from you for recycling. Many merchants are willing to collect themselves if you produce more than 1 tonne of paper a week (roughly equivalent to two or three average car boot loads). They will be particularly interested in the higher grades of waste such as computer paper or printers offcuts which can attract quite high prices - at the moment around £80 per tonne for the highest qualities. Large quantities of waste packaging paper can also be sold especially if there's a regular, guaranteed supply. Many waste paper merchants are prepared to discuss collection arrangements and prices, and may consider favourable terms for charities. Look them up in the telephone directory under Waste Paper. Organise a system of collection in offices, photocopying rooms and computer labs which separates computer waste and photocopier paper from other waste, using different clearly marked bins - making sure no other waste creeps in, such as paper clips and plastic. Appoint yourself Recycling Coordinator, organise a staff meeting, and draw office cleaners into the changes you make.

Using recycled paper

High quality paper is not necessary for many uses - loo rolls, memo pads and notebooks can all be of recycled paper. Basic office stationery, envelopes and letter head paper from recycled material now competes well in terms of price and quality with virgin paper products (contact Paperback wholesale recycled paper suppliers, for a quote - they deliver within a 100-mile radius from London or will be able to suggest suppliers local to you). High quality recycled paper is becoming increasingly popular for letterhead and printing uses - as printers gradually lose old prejudices against recycled paper. Recycled photocopying paper is available and compatible with most machines. You should check with the manufacturer and service engineer to make sure. (Rank Xerox refuse to issue warranty for use of recycled paper in their machines - they supply virgin copier paper themselves - they could be pioneering high grade recycled paper - if you are a big user ask them.)

Substantial savings can be made through a review of your organisation's paper use - you could reduce paper and envelope use; match paper quality more closely to intended use; and you could even obtain an income by selling your waste paper. The Department of Environment has saved £4000 in one year by switching to recycled stationery. A report recently considered by Islington Borough Council in London estimated that savings of almost £3000 a year could be made by using recycled paper for copying and printing purposes.

Specify use of recycled paper whenever you can - when printing newsletters, books, and drawing-up design briefs. The Body Shop actively demands the use of recycled paper in all its printed material. When you use recycled paper products let people know - print it at the bottom of your letterhead - help give recycled paper use a positive image. This book is printed on 100 % recycled Sylvancoat paper with a Speckletone recycled coverboard.

Growing trees

The savings that you make by reducing your consumption of virgin paper and putting your waste to good use, you could use for caring for and growing trees. If you only have a small balcony you can grow many small trees. Where you have more space there will be a greater opportunity to improve your working surroundings. Car parks can be refreshed with trees which will shade the cars in the summer. Instead of large areas of grass why not plant a small wood or fence an area and let it regenerate - much more pleasant for leisurely lunch time strolls and sandwiches. Well-placed groups of trees will reduce noise from busy roads, absorb pollutants in the air and could mean lower heating and air conditioning bills! Why not commission a sculptor or craftsperson to make some seats of local materials echoing the spirit of the place. Common Ground and the Woodland Trust with local councils and regional arts associations has commissioned a number of "country seats" for local people to use and enjoy.

Further reading

Pippa Hyam, 1988, Setting Up a Waste Paper Collection Scheme in the Office, Friends of the Earth - Recycling Unit,
Brian Clouston & Kathy Stansfield, (eds), 1981, Trees in Towns, Architectural Press
FoE, 1988, Good Wood Guide

IN PARKS AND HOSPITAL GROUNDS

Parks

Parks are often monotonous and uninteresting because they are over-tidy. Interest, variety and wild life could be brought to your local park if only nature is given the chance.

Old trees can provide a source of seed and a focus around which an area could simply be left alone by the lawn mowers and the trees allowed to regenerate naturally. There is evidence to suggest that saplings without stakes attract less vandalism. Contact the leisure/ recreation department of the district or borough council encourage them to adopt a light-handed approach, make them see this as a positive action - which will save time and money. Obtain local support for such a project, talk to the park keepers - very often they hear only complaints. Ask them to take a more relaxed attitude to misshapen, damaged or diseased and fallen trees - they will add character to the park and act as reminders of local events. Ensure they use their gang-mowers sensitively - many trees are killed by careless driving.

Suggest to the park keepers that they allow ivy to grow up a few of the park trees. Ivy does little harm to trees and provides nesting places and food for birds. It will also reduce the formal and sterile appearance of the park.

Set up a Local Park Users group. Invite councillors and the parks management team along to meetings. Excite park keepers with the idea of involving local people, schools and other groups, in caring for the park. This should reduce damage and may help to attract more resources from the council. You could write a leaflet or produce a newsletter about the trees in the park - look into their history, what types there are, how they come to be there, how they are looked after and any new projects. Distribute copies of the leaflet to local tenants and residents' associations, amenity groups and schools - publicise it in the local newspapers and on the radio.

Ensure that any new planting is in keeping with the character of the park and its history. Involve the people who use the park in choosing the trees and organising the planting.

Hospital Grounds

Anyone who has spent time in hospital or ill in bed knows what a pleasure it is to see even the smallest hint of greenery - flowers and trees. Studies in the U.S. show that patients with a window view of trees spent less time in hospital, required less attention from nurses and had fewer complications.

Trees and woods are wonderful to stroll through, rest and find peace in for recuperating patients and worried visitors, not to mention fraught doctors, nurses and other workers. Get the head of the

DIVIDED

Occupational Therapy Unit involved. The therapeutic benefit of closeness to trees and the natural world can extend beyond passive appreciation. When patients are physically capable, practical involvement in caring for and growing trees can be beneficial and rewarding. In West Sussex mentally handicapped patients of Lantern House have been involved in coppicing local woods and marketing the produce.

Most people from Lantern House worked in the woodland at some time, but on a regular basis a team of four to six residents and one or two staff (usually volunteers) worked for two days a week. The following season the project bought 3/4 acre of chestnut coppice (as standing timber). A similar work pattern was maintained, but coppicing offered more opportunities for residents to do some felling using bowsaws....the whole team was dragging felled timber, cutting to length, staking, removing brush....the cut timber was used mainly for fencing stakes, bean poles and peasticks...

(John Vincent, Lantern House, 1987)

Deciduous trees are well-suited to the often extensive grounds of hospitals, nursing homes as well as to small gardens of the permanently disabled - the seasonal changes are more obvious, they

OAKS

blossom, provide colour and attract more wild life. Consider establishing a small orchard in your hospital - just a few fruit trees can be grown in more restricted spaces. Fruit has medicinal values which can help recuperation. Many varieties of apple are particularly high in Vitamin C - including Beauty of Bath, Orleans Reinette and Ribstone Pippin (each of these has three times more Vitamin C than Golden Delicious). (There's even an apple, thought to have long since disappeared, called the English Hospital Reinette, which was found growing in the last century in an old hospital near Thorne in Yorkshire.)

A local conservation group should be able to help and may be willing to undertake looking after the area. An old orchard in hospital grounds in the London Borough of Redbridge is currently being resuscitated by the London Wildlife Trust. Horticultural Therapy an organisation which provide advice and training for occupational therapists, also publishes various leaflets on gardening for and with disabled and ill people. Grants may be available for tools, material and survey costs from the Royal Society for Nature Conservation and UK2000, who are jointly running a project to promote Hospital Wildlife Gardens. Write to the RSNC for details.

Find out what your local hospital or health authority are doing to care for trees in the hospital grounds. Talk to the grounds staff and District Works Manager and encourage them to extend and improve opportunities for wild life to flourish around the hospital. When new development is planned or old hospitals closed down, ensure existing trees and wild areas are retained. Seek Tree Preservation Orders to make sure.

Further reading/information

RSNC/UK2000, 1988, Hospital Wildlife Gardens - A Project Pack
Chris Baines, 1986, The Wild Side of Town, Elm Tree Books. Chapter on 'urban woodlands'.
Horticultural Therapy, Goulds Ground, Vallis Way, Frome, Somerset BA11 3DW - leaflets include 'Growing Trees from Seed and Cuttings', 'Woodland Work and Activities' and 'Greenwood Skills'.

TREES AND DEVELOPMENT

New development - housing, offices, industrial - is a rapacious threat to trees. Many trees every year are needlessly swept away by bulldozers or simply killed by ignorance, to make way for new buildings - which are more often than not accompanied by newly planted saplings!

The retention of mature trees and hedgerows is very important where development is proposed in parkland, gardens or woodland because this:
- lessens the visual intrusion of new development
- lessens the impact of construction work - noise, dust particles and so on.
- adds maturity to new buildings, enabling them to blend in with surroundings
- maintains the character and attractiveness
- creates an immediate presence
- provides continuity of wild life habitat
- adds to value of the area.

Tree protection

Keep an eye out for vacant, uncared for buildings and derelict areas with trees, or any areas that you know are due to be developed - check to ensure the trees are protected by a Tree Preservation Order (TPO). If they are not, ask the council to issue an Order as soon as possible.

If a tree or group of trees protected by a T.P.O. is affected by a development proposal then this must be taken into account by the Local Planning Authority in deciding whether to give planning permission. There are cases where planning permission for development has been refused on the grounds of the loss or potential loss of protected or valuable trees.

Village Trees Vital to Scene

Felling trees to make way for a proposed 2-bedroomed house would seriously affect the character of Five Ashes a DoE Inspector decided. He has dismissed an appeal against refusal of planning permission for a house on land adjoining Edstone Cottage. Following written representations and an inspection of the site the Inspector said he was convinced the loss of any protected trees on the site would be highly detrimental to both the appearance and character of the northern end of the village....

(Kent and Sussex Courier, 3/2/89.)

....Another important factor which I consider lends weight to my conclusions, concerns the particular belt of frontage trees along Pin Hill. These trees in my view are a significant feature of the attractive appearance of the site...I share the council's opinion that the appeal scheme would likely result in the loss of a significant number of those roadside trees and that this would seriously harm the appearance of these surroundings.

(An extract from a recent Inspector's report refusing planning permission for a new development on the outskirts of Exeter.)

Good practice

If planning permission is given however, an existing T.P.O. is automatically overridden. In this case it is important to ensure that the council impose conditions on the development which allow for the retention of existing trees, their protection during construction work and which make provision for planting new ones. Where new planting is proposed after construction is completed, insist to the council that they require this to be in harmony with existing trees. Find out if your council has a code of practice relating to the protection of trees on development sites - if they don't encourage them to adopt one and ensure that it is enforced. Hertfordshire County Council have issued guidelines on 'The Landscape of Building Developments', containing information on how to prevent damage to trees during construction and creating new landscapes.

Some buildings have been built with a particular tree or group of trees in mind. The original Crystal Palace entirely enclosed a large elm tree. The New Victoria Theatre in Stoke-on-Trent was designed around the mature trees and its car park is criss-crossed by new hedge banks. Where new buildings are proposed demand they be

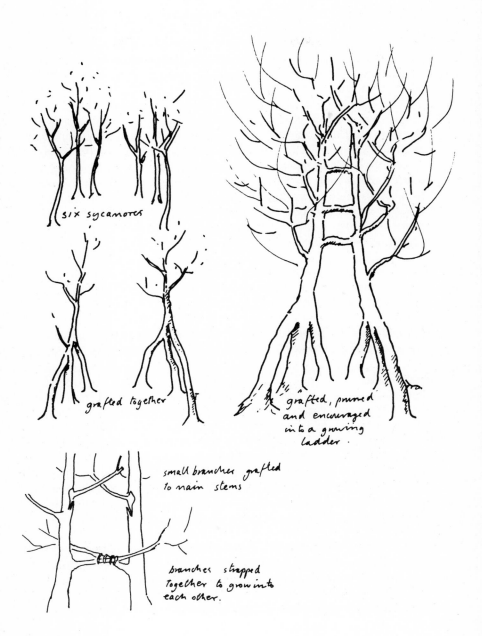

six sycamores

grafted together

grafted, pruned
and encouraged
into a growing
ladder.

small branches grafted
to main stems

branches strapped
together to grow into
each other.

designed around existing trees. There are many examples of good practice - the designs for housing layouts for Welwyn Garden City in the 1930's, aimed to preserve as many existing trees as possible. (Edwards, 1981) Today the New Homes Marketing Board run the Green Leaf Awards which hope to encourage a more sensitive approach to building.

Where large-scale development works are proposed a landscape architect should conduct a survey of trees on the site for developers - indicating how trees can best be retained. This should be done before architect's proposals are drawn-up. The tree survey should ensure as far as possible that there will be no conflict between future users of the development and the trees. Make sure that the proposed buildings do not constitute an overdevelopment of the area that will threaten the future of retained trees. You could use this argument to have plans modified or even turned down.

It is important that both old and mature trees and young saplings are retained to provide a mixed age structure. Younger trees may be better able to withstand any disturbance during construction work. Groups of trees and small areas of woodland should be kept as far as possible as this is better for wild life and better aesthetically, as well as offering a variety of leisure uses.

Enforcement

Many agreements can be reached on paper but the trees are not safe unless the plans and principles for the retention are put into practice. Site managers and workers must be fully informed and persuaded of proposals for keeping trees. There are a number of ways trees can be protected before construction work begins:
- trees being retained should be clearly and securely marked with brightly coloured tape/ribbon
- all intrusion under the canopy of trees should be prevented, especially excavation, movement and parking of vehicles, making fires, disposal of chemicals and stacking building materials - to avoid soil compaction - which damages roots and impedes drainage. This is best achieved by erecting a strong chestnut pale fence at least 5 feet high, around the area covered by the tree canopy.
- where fencing is not possible, the trunk and bark of the tree should

be protected by timber offcuts or chestnut paling.

Very often the council will not be able to enforce planning conditions or good site practice as much as it would like. Keep a look out yourself for potentially damaging practices and report them to the site manager and tree officer - demand fines for any damage to protected trees - but better build up a rapport with the workers and site manager - they'll be more likely to take care next time too.

Under the 1971 Town and Country Planning Act, the council can enter into a Section 52 Agreement with a developer to ensure trees are protected. This is a stronger measure than a planning condition and is legally binding. Ask your council to consider making a Section 52 Agreement when valued trees are threatened by development.

Further reading

Helliwell, D.R, 1985, Trees on Development Sites, Arboricultural Association
Lambeth B.C., Protection of Trees on Development Sites
Herts County Council, Guidelines on the Landscape of Building Developments
Information about Green Leaf Awards from the New Homes Marketing Board, 82 New Cavendish Street, London W1M 8AD
Edwards, A., 1981, The Design of Suburbia, Pembridge Press Ltd.

TREES AND BUILDINGS

I suspect some religious element in my feeling towards woods. Their mysterious atmospheres, their silences. The parallels - especially in beechwoods - with columned naves that Baudelaire seized on in his famous line about a temple of living pillars, all these must recall the man-made holy place. We know that the very first holy places in Neolithic times, long before Stonehenge (which is only a petrified copse), were artificial wooden groves made of felled, transported and re-erected tree trunks...

(John Fowles, 1979, The Tree)

In A Nutshell

Trees and architecture

Trees and woods have inspired architectural designs throughout the centuries. Columns and roof arches are direct references to the trunks and branches of trees. The connection between trees and architecture is perhaps most apparent in our gothic cathedrals, such as Wells and Canterbury.

Magnificent trees complement some of the finest buildings in town and country - and frequently hide the ugliest monstrosity. In London the plane tree complements majestically many buildings and is particularly at home in the Georgian Squares where it was planted when the buildings were being constructed. In the same way carefully grown or planted trees can add beauty and scale to your own house or office. In windy places trees have been planted as shelter for centuries and current research is encouraging energy saving planting again.

Problems with trees

Despite the happy coexistence of trees and buildings for centuries, fears are expressed about the problems and dangers of trees growing near buildings. These are frequently unfounded and often wildy exaggerated. Recently these fears owe a lot to conditions during the summer drought of 1976 and after the freak winds of the past few years. During the drought many buildings suffered structural problems - subsidence, cracks in brickwork and damage to foundations. In many cases trees were blamed for causing or exacerbating such damage - their roots seeking out and extracting limited moisture from soils, thus causing them to shrink. The causes of damage to buildings were subsequently found to be more complex including other factors such as poor building foundations and clay soils.

Damage to buildings by trees is only likely to be caused during unusual climatic conditions - and even then only when located on what are called shrinkable clay soils (not all clays shrink); and where the tree has a large water demand. Other reasons for damage might be frost; vibration - from transport - near main roads and airports; subsidence due to mining, or simply bad workmanship. In London it is unusual to find older buildings which show no subsidence. The buildings tend to accommodate the continual expansion and contraction of clay soils which happens with or without trees.

Solutions

Problems of trees being too close to buildings can be avoided by ensuring that foundations are adequate and appropriate to soil conditions. An adequately founded building on clay soils should present no problems when trees are planted nearby. If you live on clay soils prone to shrinking you can put your mind at rest by planting trees with a low water demand such as birch, holly, mulberry and pines; avoiding those with high water demand such as poplar, alder, willow and oak; and by planting trees at a suitable distance from buildings. The Building Research Establishment suggest a safe distance for oak and poplar on highly shrinkable clay soils as being equivalent to the maximum expected height of the tree. Other trees, including lime, ash, plane and birch can safely grow at a distance of half the expected maximum height of the tree. Many old trees and houses happily co-exist within feet of each other.

Removal not the answer

If you suspect a tree might be responsible for structural damage, after having checked the type of soil and state of foundations, removal of the tree might not be the answer. It could even exacerbate the problem by causing the soil to swell or heave to compensate for the reduction in the water demand. In this case judicious pruning of the tree, perhaps pollarding might be the appropriate course, keeping a check on the growth of the tree above and below ground and therefore its water requirements. Trees pollarded in the recent past should be kept pollarded otherwise this might upset the balance between the tree and building. Underpinning of the foundations might be a solution.

Seek advice from the local building control officer if you are unsure about incidence of structural problems associated with soil type in your locality. Don't always take the word of Insurance Companies - many are over-cautious and unqualified to make judgements about complex cases - seek a second opinion from a building surveyor, structural engineer or a recommended arboriculturalist all with local experience.

New house purchasers have a responsibility to the place they move into and any trees there may be. They should not be allowed to remove trees which have been an asset to a place for years. Before you move on get a TPO placed on your tree - if this isn't possible consider inserting a restrictive covenant in the deeds.

Further reading

Tony Aldous (ed), 1979, Trees and Buildings , RIBA Publication Ltd
Cutler, D.F., and Richardson, I.B.K., 1981, Tree Roots and Buildings, Construction Press
Hall, THR, 1979, Trees and Buildings, Arboricultural Association
Hebblethwaite. RL, 1980 The Conservation of Trees and Shrubs in Built-up Areas, Devon Trust for Nature Conservation
Building Research Establishment, 1985, Digest 298 The Influence of Trees on House Foundations in Clay Soils

TREES AND POLLUTION

"I needed lungs" said the tree "and my sap turned to leaves so that I might breathe, my leaves fell and I did not die. My fruit contains all my thoughts on life."

(Andre Gide, 1952, The Fruits of the Earth)

Trees of Life

Without trees there would be no life. Trees help us breathe. The use and exchange of atmospheric gases by trees is essential to our survival and the survival of all nature. Trees are nature's air conditioning units, they produce oxygen - a single mature beech can provide enough oxygen in a day to supply the needs of at least 4 people - grow wood, and soak up in the process carbon dioxide which is a major contributor to the greenhouse effect and consequent global warming.

Trees act as humidifiers - refreshing and cooling the air. Mature trees release huge quantities of water - a beech can transpire up to 100 gallons a day in summer. You can freshen your house or office by planting trees near by - they will also reduce noise and increase privacy.

They also remove unwanted dust particles from the air by trapping them on leaves, to be washed down in the following rainfall - two and a half acres of beechwood can extract about 4 tonnes of dust from the atmosphere each year. Trees will also encourage the deposition of lead from car exhaust fumes. It has been estimated that the rate of accumulation of lead in soil under trees is twice as much as under grass in the open.

For more than a century we have been pumping noxious fumes into the atmosphere at a dramatic rate. We now know that we must take urgent action to improve the air we share with trees. Where better to start than by roads - the major source of deadly pollutants.

About 9,000 tonnes of lead is added to our petrol each year. Of this, some 60-70% (6,500 tonnes) is emitted into the atmosphere, a significant propor-

tion being deposited on motorway verges. The majority of lead pollution is concentrated within a zone of some 50m (55 yards) on either side of the motorway. Only 10-30% extends outwards as far as 100m.

(Dowdeswell, 1987)

Trees and roads

Grow trees and hedges along roads to shelter fields, gardens and allotments from pollutants such as lead which can enter plants grown for food and be dangerous to health. Where there are quite large roadside verges you can encourage natural regeneration - particularly if the verge borders on a woodland - a ready source of seed. Roadside trees and woods will reduce wind speeds. They can also break up the monotony of long journeys - and will be of added interest if you grow trees appropriate to the character of your locality. The Forestry Commission through its District Offices already plants between 1.5 and 2 million trees along motorways and trunk roads under contract to the Department of Transport. Other roads are usually the responsibility of the county council who act as Highways Authority. Ask the council tree officer if you can have more trees planted along roads in your neighbourhood. Your parish council is able to plant trees on roadside verges as long as it

has approval from the Highways Authority. Suggest they do this. As part of your parish tree map - identify all existing roadside trees and look for areas where they can be extended and new ones planted.

Encouraging trees and woods to grow along roadsides can be beneficial in many respects but this doesn't tackle the problem at source. Pollutants from cars and lorries can harm trees. Motor vehicles are responsible for almost half the total emissions of nitrogen oxide in Britain, one of the main pollutants causing acid rain - which is thought to damage stressed trees. Combined with hydrocarbons, nitrogen oxide also produces ozone which is poisonous to trees.

Reduce pollution damage to trees by walking more, and using public transport wherever possible. If you drive, keep your speed down - this reduces the amount of pollution you cause. There is little excuse these days for not using unleaded petrol - CLEAR have prepared a list of all the cars which can use unleaded petrol with no or simply minor modifications, and where unleaded petrol is being sold. It may cost as little as £15 to convert your car. When you buy a new car ensure it has a catalytic convertor fitted, this will reduce emissions of nitrogen oxide, carbon monoxide and hydrocarbons.

Air quality

Find out how good your air is - contact the environmental health department of the district or borough council who should monitor daily levels of air pollution, ask for more information. You might live in a designated Smoke Control Area where it is illegal to burn unauthorised fuels such as bituminous coal or wood. Don't burn leaves - compost them for use in your garden or allotment. Alert your environmental health officer if you suspect any contravention of the regulations. If you don't live in a smoke control area lobby the council to designate one.

Major industries - power stations, cement works - are controlled by Her Majesty's Inspectorate of Pollution which has District Inspectors in local offices around the country. Look in the telephone directory for the nearest office. If you are concerned about emissions from large plants complain to the District Inspector.

Certain trees are also susceptible to salts used to de-ice roads - find out what the council uses, ask them to use grit as an alternative. Don't let them dump piles of road salt near trees or hedges. Trees are affected both by soil contamination and aerial deposition. Some types of tree are more tolerant than others to salt - grey and goat willow, sea buckthorn and hawthorn are all relatively tolerant; but many of our common trees including beech, maples, limes and chestnuts suffer badly from salt pollution.

Further reading

Dowdeswell, W.H., 1987, Hedgerows and Verges, Allen and Unwin
Fred Pearce, 1987, Acid Rain, Penguin
CLEAR, Campaign for Lead Free Air,
National Society for Clean Air have a number of leaflets - including 1989, 'Air Pollution - Know Your Rights', 1987, 'Lead and You - reducing the risks' and 'Clean Air Begins At Home'
Chris Rose, 1988, Acid Rain - it's happening here, Greenpeace
Ling, K.A., and Ashmore, M.R., 1988, Acid Rain and Nature Conservation in Britain, NCC

IN CHURCHYARDS AND CEMETERIES

Old Yew, which graspest at the stones
That name the under-lying dead,
Thy fibres net the dreamless head,
Thy roots are wrapt about the bones.....

Alfred Lord Tennyson

There is a close relationship between woods and churches as places of worship and refuge. Churchyards, in town and country, provide a sanctuary for trees, especially old trees, as well as people, both living and long since departed. Some trees growing in churchyards may actually pre-date the buildings themselves. As Francesca Greenoak says, "Trees possibly do more than any other plants to

CHURCH YARD YEW

create the atmosphere of a churchyard. Without them churchyards are almost invariably bleak and windswept - small plains without any points of reference".

Yew trees

Yew, one of our few native evergreens, is the traditional churchyard tree. They are often the oldest living things in our landscape. Some are over 1000 years old and were planted on sacred sites as symbols of immortality and as a protective spirit. In Woolland Churchyard, Dorset the yew measures over 31 feet around its girth. They have been planted singly, in small groups, avenues and in circles suggesting origins more ancient than the church itself. The yew is steeped with religious and spiritual association and meaning. All churchyard yews should be protected by a Tree Preservation Order (TPO) - they are valuable for wild life, providing a secure winter haven, and an excellent breeding place for birds including the mistle thrush, chaffinch and goldcrest. Don't cut down a yew just because it is hollow or shows no external signs of life - they have been known to burst back to life after several years dormancy.

The Cedar of Lebanon and holly are two more evergreens which are also often found in churchyards. The red berries of both holly and yew are believed powerful against evil and are particularly attractive to birds. Oak, beech, lime, horse chestnut, rowan and thorn are all associated with churchyards. Tall trees such as beech and lime often support extensive rookeries. Hawthorn is held to be a sacred tree.

Caring for churchyard trees

In addition to protection afforded by a TPO, the consent of the Diocesan Parsonages Board must be sought before any trees in churchyards are felled. You can obtain their address from the Parochial Church Council (PCC) - contact the Board if there is a proposal to fell trees with which you disagree. Talk to the local vicar if you are unhappy about any work on churchyard trees.

Encourage the local vicar and churchgoers to care for existing trees and to adopt a more relaxed attitude to looking after the churchyard.

The PCC which looks after many of the church's affairs are usually responsible for care of the churchyard. Ask them to leave small areas to regenerate naturally. If any tree has produced small seedlings, selected ones could be left alone to grow. Create a hedge with hazel, holly and hawthorn to mark the perimeter of the churchyard. You could also introduce shrubs such as guelder rose and dogwood in corners. Elsewhere the grass only needs to be cut twice a year in July and mid autumn, leaving cowslips, primroses and bulbs undisturbed to seed. Ask them to inform and consult local people through church noticeboard or parish magazine, about the trees and any proposed work. Let it be known that the churchyard is valued for its trees, encourage them to allow more to grow.

The Nature Conservancy Council has recently produced an information pack on conservation in churchyards and also provide grants for churchyard projects which will enhance wild life. Your county trust for nature conservation will be able to provide advice - obtain its address from the telephone directory.

Cemeteries

Victorian cemeteries, are well known places of beauty and are important for trees and wild life in many of our cities. As a result of lack of resources and the power of nature many have subsequently become self-sown woodlands. Many magnificent specimen trees, including Gingko and Turkey oak add to their interest. In Brighton, Woodvale cemetery harbours a valuable collection of many different sorts of elm. Abney Park Cemetery in Stoke Newington, with its distinctive pollarded poplars, was actually planned as an arboretum with 2,500 varieties of trees and shrubs. Set-up a Friends group for your local churchyard or cemetery, organise walks, picnics and talks about its trees and wild life.

Further reading

Stapleton, H, & Burnam, P.,1976, The Churchyard's Handbook, CIO
David Goode, 1986, Wild in London, Michael Joseph Ltd.
Francesca Greenoak, 1985, God's Acre, Orbis
Cornish, V., 1946, The Churchyard Yew and Immortality, Muller
NCC/UK2000, 1989, The Living Churchyard,

Chapter 3 - **PROJECTS**

ADOPT-A-TREE

Whilst most trees carry on the work of millennia without our help, any tree clearly in trouble must be cared for. Planted trees will need particular care in the first few years after planting. Trees in the country and in towns have to put up with an array of threats and dangers. Often the council are not able to spare the necessary time and resources to look after street trees as much as they would like.

The most immediate way you can begin to help trees is by adopting one and deciding that you are going to care for it. Most of the time this will simply mean creating conditions for the tree to flourish on its own. There may however be occasions when a tree suffers damage due to the hazards of living in a town - knocks by cars and lorries, vandalism and pollution. You are in the best position to keep an eye on a tree near your home, work or school. Report any major damage to your local tree or arboricultural officer. Discuss with them what help you can offer. To start with you could water the tree regularly during dry periods, remove unwanted growth - such as suckers - around ground level, loosen ties which may be strangling the tree, and be alert to any intentional damage or disease. Take registration numbers of vehicles which damage trees in your street and report them to the tree officer.

Ask your local council to start an **adopt-a-tree** scheme in your area. In Camden, London, a number of trees have been adopted along the Greenways route, a green corridor of streets linking Lincoln's Inn Fields with King's Cross. Growth Unlimited, who are promoting the scheme with the council, have produced a useful booklet, 'Adopt-a-street-tree - a community approach to care of urban street trees'; which outlines the types of tree planted; their history; appropriate trees to plant; why it is important to care for street trees and what care they require. (send sae for booklet to Growth Unlimited, Voluntary Action Camden, 25/31 Tavistock Place, London, WC1H 9SE).

If you don't already have a tree near you to adopt try to get one planted. Some councils have a tree sponsorship project whereby local people or businesses on payment of a small sum, can have a tree planted for them. If you want trees in your street, join together with neighbours and approach the tree officer. Let your local councillor know. Don't take no for an answer. Make sure you choose a tree which fits in with the character of your neighbourhood. In the summer of 1988 Runnymede Borough Council, Surrey, wrote to all local community groups, schools, residents groups and park users, offering to pay half the costs where people wish to sponsor the planting of a tree. In determining the price of tree-sponsorship some councils add a little for the costs of after-care.

You could adopt a working wood or orchard. There may be one near your home which is not fully used or harvested. Find out who the owner is and ask if you can use it, offer to pay a small annual rent. With orchards you can then obtain your own fresh fruit locally - a fruit grower near Colchester, in Essex, has recently started such a scheme. If you gather enough local support you could establish your own community orchard or working woodland.

In A Nutshell

Further reading

Greenways leaflet, 1988, 'Adopt-a-Street-Tree - a community approach to care of urban street trees'.

Set of 6 - Practical Action postcards on Tree Care and Conservation - by Common Ground, 45 Shelton Street, London WC2H 9HJ (£1.50 for set of six).

TREE FESTIVALS AND CELEBRATIONS

There are myriad exciting and enjoyable ways - writing, drama, dance, yearly festivals - in which you can begin to express the value of trees in your locality. Many people all over the world celebrate the indispensible, life-giving role of trees.

In 'The Golden Bough' Sir James Fraser explores how the worship of trees is embedded in different cultures throughout the world, many of which stem from ancient religious beliefs. In India a number of trees, including the fig tree, is considered sacred. Peach blossom is used in annual ceremonies in China. In Britain the may-pole is the centrepoint of an ancient may-day festival to celebrate the annual rebirth of nature, often featuring a green man, jack-in-the-green or figure clothed in leaves.

Fraser writes,

In spring or early summer or even on Midsummer day, it was and still is in many parts of Europe the custom to go out to the woods, cut down a tree and bring it into the village, where it is set up amid general rejoicings... The intention of these customs is to bring home to the village and each house, the blessings which the tree-spirit has in its power to bestow.

The precise origin and meaning of many customs have been lost in time. In Aston-on-Clun, Shropshire, a black poplar tree in the village centre is permanently bedecked with flags which are renewed in an ancient annual ceremony. Wassailing the apple trees is a traditional ceremony which takes place on Twelfth Night, where local people - farmers, friends, neighbours, and farm workers - gather around the most productive tree in the orchard to sing and toast its health and encourage a good harvest in the coming year. Cider is drunk and parts of the tree, roots and branches are bathed in the liquid. Different local versions of wassailing songs were used in Somerset, Herefordshire and Gloucestershire.

Celebration can be more closely associated with protest and protection of trees. The Chipko Andolan movement of Uttar Pradesh, India has grown out of a spontaneous protest by local women in 1974 against proposed commercial felling in local forests. Chipko means to hug and the movement took its name from the practice of hugging the trees which the women used to prevent the contractors from felling them. The Chipko movement now spans the whole Himalayan region. More than a protest movement, the tree-huggers celebrate the value of the trees, praising the forest with song and argue their case for the vital role of trees in the local economy and in preventing erosion.

If you know of old festivals in your own locality which celebrate nature, you could revive them and renew their significance. Make links with existing trees and woods in your parish and develop new ways to express the local meaning and value they embody. Writing can be a powerful medium of expressing the importance of our surroundings. You could research writing - poetry and essays - about your locality and its trees. The local library is a good place to start. Compile an anthology of writings about local trees. Encourage new writing, poetry or even a play. Excite local writing groups or evening classes and the local newspaper in the idea. You might be able to interest a local publisher in helping you.

In 1985 West Midland Arts and Common Ground cooperated in setting up a writing scheme whereby local groups could commission a local writer to create new work in response to the local environment, and particularly its trees and woods. A collection of new poems which "celebrate nature as it survives and beautifies the city and the spiritual and cultural tradtions of trees, woods and the green man we have inherited from ancient times" by Heather Harrison; and a collection of essays and letters by Bill Laws have so far been published, and Eleanor Cooke's work on Prees Heath filled a half hour Kaleidoscope programme on Radio 4.

There are many opportunities to explore the multi-cultural richness of our relationships with trees and each other: Theatr Taleisin linked Celtic and Indian people, music, stories and dance to create a cross cultural performance called 'The Tree of Life'.

You could devise a play around local trees of distinction or the oldest trees in your locality. In 1987 Theatre of the Heart performed the 'World Tree' on Hampstead Heath. Three separate journeys through the heath, actors leading audience, drew attention to interesting and unusual trees to be found there. Draw attention to the value and beauty of trees in your locality by celebrating them. This way we make it harder for them to be destroyed.

Further reading

Eleanor Cooke, (in press), Who Killed Prees Heath, West Midlands Arts/Common Ground
Heather Harrison, 1987, Roots Beneath the Pavement, Birmingham Readers and Writers Festival
Bill Laws, 1987, Common Losses, Birmingham Readers and Writers Festival
A. Porteous, 1928, Forest Folklore and Mythology and Romance, Allen and Unwin
Sir J.G. Frazer, 1987, The Golden Bough, Papermac

Two old pollard willows

LANDMARK AND BOUNDARY TREES

Trees locate us in time and place. They have always been useful as a means of telling us where we are - as direction markers, helping us find our way and as boundary markers.

In the open country, a farmer who wanted to let the drovers know that he was able to provide food, accomodate and grazing, planted 3 Scots pines. These were visible at a great distance and the drovers used them as way marks. When they reached England, they found that groups of yew trees served the same purpose. These trees remain where all traces of the old inns or farms have disappeared.....

(Fay Godwin and Shirley Toulson, 1977)

They have proven such potent landmarks that many of our place-names still convey their lasting importance, such as May Tree Hill and Five Ashes.

In A Nutshell

Thorndon...was situated in a dense jungle of Black and possibly White thorn which sloped down to a freshwater lake... Very interesting information concerning the early geography of our immediate landscape is supplied by the names of adjoining villages, confirming the fact that it was a vast forest variegated with jungle, swamp and heathland. Adjoining us is Thornham (the hamlet in the thorns), Thwaite (a clearing), Occold and Oakley (oaks), Stoke Ash (the stockaded ash....Brome (Broom), Aspal (aspen), and of the marsh we have Rishangles (Rush hangar).

(Mr. Harris, vicar of Thorndon, East Suffolk, in V. Cornish, 1944)

Individual trees have for a long time acted as a means of marking out territory. At Haileybury in Hertfordshire, Quitchell's Oak marks one corner of St. Margaret's parish and was first mentioned over 350 years ago. Early Saxon charters frequently mention individual trees. Sometime during the ninth or tenth century a description was made of the land around Crediton - or 'Creedy-land' as it was then known, in Devon. 78 landmarks are recorded in the area, many of which are trees:

..from Cyrtla's gate to the crab-apple tree. From the crab-apple tree to the Green Way....from the path straight to the alder...From the precipice to the head of the birch-combe...Thence to Broad Ash. From the alder-thicket to the landslip.
(quoted in Finberg, 1969, West Country Historical Studies)

More recent tithe maps record and identify particular trees on points along parish boundaries.

A place-name often to be found (if no longer with its revered oak tree) on parish boundaries, a fossil from the medieval festival observed on the Rogation Days, or Cross Days, immediately before Ascension Day. A procession was formed. Crossed and green boughs and flowers were carried around the parish, the boundaries of the parish land were noted and confirmed, crosses were traced on the ground, and at recognised stopping places, such as an oak, the priest read the scriptures and invoked divine blessings on the land and crops. There are many more boundary names of the same origin such as Gospel Thorn, Amen Corner.

(Geoffrey Grigson,1982)

Research your boundaries. The county/borough record office will have estates maps and tithe maps which show the old bounds. Find out if they've been changed in recent years. You might locate old boundaries that are full of interest - historical, cultural and ecological. A few hedges which once formed part of a continuous area of woodland, remain as boundary markers left over after periodic clearances of the wood which once stretched over the whole country. These can be over 1000 years old. In Dulwich, south London, ancient field boundary oaks still grow among newly built houses.

Many similar areas in towns provide evidence of the fields beneath (see Tindall, 1977; Neville, 1987).

Identify trees which act as important landmarks in your locality. Make sure they are protected by a Tree Preservation Order. Let whoever owns the trees know how much you value them. Revive the annual beating of the bounds - it can be an enjoyable community event and will draw attention to the importance of boundary trees.

Create new landmark trees. By doing this you can add interest to the landscape and say something about the values of the present community to future generations. Approach the landholder of a focal point in your parish and suggest the idea. Restore the oak to the Royal Oak pub and the ash to Knotty Ash. Obtain the support of the parish or borough council. Ask them to consider growing trees along the parish boundary to mark out your home-patch. If a local tithe map records the type of tree on a boundary try growing the same. The Rossington Environment Association, South Yorkshire, with the help of local landowners and schools, have so far planted more than 1,000 trees along the boundary which is 10 miles long. Clumps of trees and small woodlands also act as landmarks - for example the beech rings of Chanctonbury and Cissbury on the South Downs are well known and can be seen for miles. Avenues of trees such as those at Badbury rings and Pamphill in Dorset, bring mysterious and enchanting atmosphere to a place. Landmark trees help us orientate and identify with particular places. The Countryside Commission provide grant-aid for the care and replacement of landmark trees such as hill-top trees and tree-lined avenues.

But be careful - some of our finest prehistoric landmarks such as hillforts and barrows are crowned with distinctive trees. Sadly tree roots are damaging buried remains (which are a vital source of knowledge from our ancestors.) Make sure you don't plant on existing earthworks or any site known to contain archaeological remains. Check with your County Site and Monuments Record at the county council offices before planting.

In Kassel, West Germany a few years ago, Joseph Beuys was invited to make a sculpture - a simple idea disguises a highly political act (Beuys was one founder of the German green party).

His sculpture consisted of 7,000 blocks of basalt arranged in a large pile. In addition, Beuys declared that he would plant 7,000 trees on public ground at Kassel and that for each tree planted, a block of basalt would be removed from the sculpture and placed beside it. The sculpture therefore consisted in its slow diminution, connected with the consciousness that whenever a stone was taken away, a tree would be planted in one of the town's districts... The political purpose of Beuys's work starts from his assumption that a well-run town should have a garden department, whose policy would be to plant trees wherever it was physically possible!

(The Unpainted Landscape, 1987)

Set up a landmark tree scheme. Be Sensitive to the locality, encourage local participation, demand public access, use locally indigenous trees, plan for after-care provision and the use of stone or other natural materials.

Further Reading

Tom Greeves, 1987, The Parish Boundary, Common Ground
Gillian Tindall, 1977, The Fields Beneath, Maurice Temple Smith
Neville, L., 1987, The Great North Wood, London Wildlife Trust
Scottish Arts Council, 1987, The Unpainted Landscape, Coracle Press
Fay Godwin and Shirley Toulson, 1977, The Drovers' Roads of Wales, Wildwood House

In A Nutshell

PARISH TREE WARDENS AND TREE GROUPS

Very often trees are damaged or cut down because no one takes responsibility for them. Get together and form a local tree group and assume the role of parish tree warden. Persuade others to join you and recognise your work. The tree group could have links with the local tenants association, amenity society or parish council.

As a warden you can keep an eye on local trees and woods. Suggest areas which can be left alone to allow woodland to develop naturally, and areas for planting new trees. You should find out which trees are in Conservation Areas and which have Tree Preservation Orders. Ask your tree officer to place orders on all unprotected trees. A tree warden could coordinate a tree-group to help spread the workload and provide continuity. Calne Civic Society in Wiltshire has recently set up a tree group which aims to "make Calne a more tree-conscious community." It was set up to stop a repeat of the felling of a much-loved, ancient oak tree to make way for new development. The group check and update TPO records, peruse all new planning applications and development proposals to ensure that trees are not threatened. They provide a useful link between the community, they have enlisted the support and help of a local school - and local tree officer.

Friends of Charnwood Forest

Since the inception of the Friends of Charnwood Forest in March, 1986, the Society has steadily grown in membership, knowhow and effect. The results encourage us to encourage other like-minded people to form their own groups.

It means discipline and hard work but it is well worth it. We were a rootless assortment of individuals who gnashed our teeth whenever another atrocity in the remorseless invasion of the countryside was committed in Charnwood Forest.

As individuals we just hadn't got round to protesting or organising a petition, and usually nothing was done at all...Finally we made a move, formed a steering committee, hammered out our aims and objectives, notified the press and called an inaugural meeting. The results were astounding - over 100 people turned up for it. We formed a committee, printed our stationery and we were in business.

We liaised with the relevant planning officers who were happy to supply us with a weekly list of planning applications to peruse - if any looked doubtful we visited the site and proceeded to make our observations....To date we have handled some 50 projects including plans for individual dwellings, felling of woodlands, heavy traffic on country lanes...protection of ancient trees,.. all within the boundaries of Charnwood Forest.

(David Thorpe, in Village Voice, Hereford & Worchester RCC, Spring 1988)

East Sussex Parish Tree Wardens - In Sussex a parish tree warden scheme has been developed by the East Sussex Woodland Forum, an organisation set up by the County Council, comprising representatives from a large number of groups including local authorities, the Forestry Commission, and Nature Conservancy Council. More than half of the parishes in the county have begun parish woodland surveys and 80 have appointed tree wardens - nominated by the parish council. The warden's role is to advise the parish council on matters relating to trees, management, planting, legal matters and tree protection. A newsletter is published regularly giving information and advice to parish tree wardens and listing useful contacts and addresses. A free Information Pack is issued to each warden containing information on legislation, and care for trees and woods.

The **Stroud Tree Workshop** is a small group of about twelve people who work together to plant trees in the locality during the weekends in the planting season:

Members arrange their own transport and use their own tools, though lifts can be arranged and tools lent. One member coordinates the collection of trees from our nursery area...by planting whips (2-3 feet high) the need for expensive stakes is eliminated...Most of the whips are bought in though some members raise trees from seed. Money is raised by asking for donations to cover the cost of the trees. No subscription fee is levied from members.

(Stroud Tree Workshop, 1989)

Further reading

East Sussex Woodland Forum, Information Pack for Tree Wardens
Leics County Council/CPRE, 1988, Parish Tree Wardens Information Pack
Calne Civic Society 1988 Tree Group - leaflet, s.a.e. to: Mrs. D. Smith, 17 North Street, Calne SN11 0HQ
Stroud Tree Workshop - leaflet, s.a.e. to: Lin Callard, The Old School House, Rushmire Hill, Wotton-under-Edge, Gloucs.

PARISH TREE MAPS, FAVOURITE AND REMARKABLE TREES

One way to stimulate interest in trees is to discover the interesting and valued trees in your parish or neighbourhood and make a map or book, recording why they are important, their value and meaning for local people. Start with the questions - what trees are important to you and why? Trees for climbing and hiding, for trysting and conker collecting will all be important to different people.

You may include the old trees in your locality, examining their links with past generations and historical events; trees from other countries, where they come from and who brought them; trees which are distinctive to your locality - the most common types and their distribution. You might also record unusual trees which are growing in strange shapes or which might have stories to tell.

Andrew Morton has produced a book on the 'Trees of Shropshire':

What this book attempts to do is to look at individual trees in Shropshire; trees that have become unique either because of their size, or their age, or because of the history and legends associated with them ...many old and remarkable trees survive and are for the most part respected by their owners. However Shropshire still hides its treasures away largely unpublicised and unsung....The Arbor Tree with its flags is the country's last surviving relic of ancient tree dressing rites possibly from Celtic times. The combination of Europe's best tree house and Britain's largest lime make the Pitchford tree unique....

But trees don't have to be special to be valued. The most vital aspect is why trees are important to local people. You could start a Favourite Tree project. Ask people to identify their favourite tree on the map and to say why it is important to them. It might be favourite because of its unusual shape, the colour of its leaves, its age or simply because of the sense of place it creates.

windshaped

Involve the local schools, tenants and residents associations. You could let people know what you are doing through the local newspaper and radio.

Be sure to show the results to the local council tree officer and other relevant people in the local authority planning department. The parish council clerk, chairman of tenants association and local councillors are all people who might be influential in any decisions made about the locality, make sure they know about your project. Tell them what is important to you and why.

The map can form the basis for tree protection in your parish. It will help you identify areas which can be left to regenerate naturally; where to plant new trees; which trees need to be protected by Tree Preservation Order's; and how to assess planning applications and other proposals for change. It can also help raise awareness amongst people of local trees and woods and when planning any other tree-related projects.

Town residents should approach their local planning authority for a map of your area. If you live in the country you could begin by looking at a large scale - 1: 25000 (2.5 inches to the mile) Ordnance Survey (OS) map. This will record woods and copses of trees and possibly distinguish conifers from broadleaved trees. Individual and smaller groups of trees will not normally be recorded. Larger scale maps 1;10000 will contain more information but are expensive and only cover a small area (25 km^2 or about 10 square miles). How far the information corresponds with what you find on the ground will be interesting.

You could record the position of trees, species and age in your selected area. The best time to look will be in summer or early autumn when full leaf cover makes identification of species much easier. Age can be estimated by measuring the circumference - about 4 ft from ground each inch roughly equals one year's growth - though where trees are growing closely together in groups or woods an inch is likely to represent more than a years growth. Height can be estimated by standing back and multiplying the height of a person standing against the trunk of the tree. If you need to use a book to help you identify difficult species a good one is Alan Mitchell's 'A Field Guide to Trees of Britain and Northern Europe'. A useful leaflet entitled, 'How to do a tree survey' is available from the Tree Council (for a stamped addressed envelope).

You could also examine the history of the woods in your parish. Older OS maps will reveal locations of woodlands which have since disappeared and might help in dating existing woods. Estate and tithe maps in County archives might also be useful sources of information. Local history libraries might have information about individual specimen trees or trees in parkland. Observation on the ground can uncover a great deal of information. The presence of certain trees such as the wild service are considered an indication of ancient woodland. Some trees, such as small-leaved lime, if found in a hedgerow, suggest a remnant of a once larger woodland area.

City streets sometimes follow field boundaries which you might be able to detect on old maps. Old hedgerow trees can often still be found growing there as evidence of 'the fields beneath'. (Tindall, 1987)

St. George's neighbourhood, a tenants and residents group in Islington, London have decided to create a parish tree map of the neighbourhood to discover more about the history of the area and to locate valued trees. It is also an excellent way of enhancing a sense of community identity. The local council tree officer is keen to collaborate and use information collected to update TPO records and decide where new trees can be planted.

You could organise tree walks around your parish or neighbourhood - to draw attention to important trees and valuable areas. Walks could take a theme - for example a historical walk, or a look at exotic species. They could be annual events lead by a tree warden or group and/or published in a leaflet to be distributed to houses/people in the neighbourhood - as well as the local planning officer and local councillors.

Common Ground and Time Out are creating a map of central London 'In Search of the Green Man' - searching out strange and interesting tales about trees and the use of wood to show how deeply intertwined our worlds are: from the 200th birthday of the plane trees in Berkeley Square to the unsolved mystery of where Sir Issac Newton took parts of the giant Maypole which once stood in the Strand; from the origin of the name Soho (possibly a hunting call from Charles II riding in the forest thereabouts) to the Mulberry trees in Spitalfields grown for the rearing of silk worms.

Further reading

Andrew Morton, 1986, Trees of Shropshire, Airlife Publications
Tree Council, How to do a Tree Survey (leaflet)
Alan Mitchell, 1974, Field Guide to the Trees of Britain and Northern Europe, Collins
Gillian Tindall, 1977, The Fields Beneath, Granada
Common Ground, In Search of the Green Man, Time Out, July 1989

TALL STORIES

Another way of celebrating old trees is to examine the events and local happenings that they might have witnessed in the past. In many cases this might be ingrained in the tree itself. In Hatfield Forest a giant pollarded beech bears the graffito 'RJ 1801' - who was RJ? How big was the tree in 1801? Great care had to be exercised in extracting timber from a wood near Brighton, completely devastated during the Great Storm in 1987. The wood was used as a military training area during the Second World War and the trees contained shrapnel form land mines, grenades and bullets. What secrets does your local wood or favourite tree keep?

There are many famous stories relating to events in the life of particular trees. For example Rupert's Elm in Henley-on-Thames, said to be the place from which one of Prince Rupert's soldiers was hung during a retreat of the Royalists after a famous battle during the Civil War. Meetings of a group of men hailed as the first trade unionists took place in the early nineteenth century under a sycamore which still grows near the village green in Tolpuddle, Dorset. The fortunes of the Carmarthen were linked with a 300 year old oak which used to grow in the centre of town. It was known as Merlin's Oak after the verse, 'When Merlin's tree shall tumble down, Then shall fall Carmarthen Town'. No catastrophe has yet befallen the town - despite the removal of the tree!

Old trees in your own locality are likely to have some incredible and humorous stories to tell, if only they could talk. Many of these trees would have started life in quite different times to those we know today - when there was no electricity, no radio or TV, no cars, not even bicycles.

Roadside trees would have seen some interesting sights. The trees themselves might have been meeting places - village parliaments, gospel oaks - and might even have been used in the past as a place to tell stories. By drawing attention to the trees and their value, you will make it harder for them to be cut down.

Organise a storytelling project. A series of workshops were organised by Mary Medlicott and Karen Tovell early in 1989:

The Tree of Life - a series of three storytelling workshops

1. SEEDS: SYMBOL AND STORY - This workshop will explore the symbol of the Tree of Life and its relationshps with storytelling. We will look at the possibility of drawing together a pool of stories about trees and at ways of getting to know them. If you have any stories which you feel may be relevant, please bring them along.

2. BRANCHING OUT: STORY AND COMMUNITY - This workshop will focus on strategies for exploring stories connected with the theme, the Tree of Life, in our own communities. It will look at ways of working on stories of trees with others, creating new stories, retelling old ones, exploring different cultures and backgrounds.

3. FRUIT: STORY AND THE SELF - This workshop will look at ways of harvesting the fruits of the theme of our own creative and emotional lives. We will explore techniques for making the stories our own and find ways in which we can contribute our individual creative skills such as painting, movement or music so that the stories can take root and grow in our own inner landscapes.

You could explore the life that your favourite old tree might have had and the stories it might have to tell. These stories could be based on fact or might be purely the product of the imagination. You might compile a diary of the tree - what it sees, hears, feels day after day, month by month. It could form the basis of a community play or local storytelling. Myth, legend and religion have strong connections with trees in most cultures. Sharing stories from different cultural backgrounds can preface a real celebration of our differences and similarities. This would be an ideal project to attract the support of the local radio and newspaper to draw in more people.

On the bank of the river he saw a tall tree: from roots to crown one half was aflame and the other green with leaves
(from The Mabinigion)

Further Reading

Angela King and Sue Clifford for Common Ground (eds), 1989, Trees Be Company - an anthology of poetry, Bristol Clasical Press.
Porteous, A., 1928, Forest Folklore, Mythology and Romance, Allen and Unwin
Jeffrey Gantz (trans.), 1976, The Mabinogion, Penguin
Kim Taplin, 1989, Pity the Tree - ateacher's guide through woods in children's literature, Common Ground
Brian Stone (trans.), 1974, Sir Gawain and the Green Knight, Penguin

PARISH AND COMMUNITY TREE NURSERIES

You don't need a great deal of land to start a parish or neigh-bourhood tree nursery, dozens of trees can be grown in pots on a balcony or in a backyard, you could easily grow as many as 100 trees in an area 10 square yards. By establishing a community tree nursery you can provide a focus for parish/neighbourhood activity.

You should grow your own trees from seed collected in the locality. Many nurseries in this country import stock from other countries because it is cheaper. By collecting seeds locally you will ensure that local varieties of trees are conserved and continue to be grown in your area. The trees are also more likely to grow well as they will be adapted to local soils and climate. Local school children could be involved in collecting and growing seeds for a tree nursery.

Ideal areas for a tree nursery include

- a small corner of a local park;
- part of the school grounds;
- a corner of a local field (with the farmer's permission);
- a little-used area on a housing estate;
- a derelict site in the neighbourhood (even if it's temporary);
- your own garden or a number of gardens in your street.

It is important to choose a place that is quite sheltered from strong winds, but which receives some sunlight. The soil should be easy to work and if possible typical of the locality. If you're starting in trays or pots you can use a compost/soil mixture. Ensure that the pots are kept well-watered and protected from frost. For good results you should ensure that the area is well fenced-off, with strong fencing and wire-mesh to exclude grazing animals.

There are many ways the trees can be used. They can be given to local schools to plant; planted in carefully selected places around your estate; in local parks and woods. Make sure the types of tree you are planting are appropriate to the chosen place. They can also be given to local people or businesses, for use in their own gardens, car parks, along busy roads or as a screening for an eyesore. You could even sell trees as a source of income to keep the nursery going.

The Devon Tree Bank - The Devon Wildlife Trust run a tree bank scheme with the support of Devon County Council -

The Aims of the Tree Bank

Many trees and hedgerows native to Devon have been lost through disease, destruction and development or agricultural change and severe weather conditions. The Tree Bank aims through education and practical conservation, to replace these losses and protect the woodland and hedgerows which support much of our wild life. This objective is achieved in a variety of ways, namely:

a) Publicising the existence of the Tree Bank and its objectives
b) Encouraging the community to collect seeds from trees and hedgerows native to Devon
c) Teaching how to raise seedlings and helping to establish nurseries for the growing of trees and shrubs
d) Seeking permanent sites for the maturing of trees and shrubs
e) Helping and advising with the transplanting and maintenance.

The Devon Tree Bank has been in existence for 5/6 years... relies upon the active participation of volunteers throughout the county who are organised on a local basis. Also, county schools are actively encouraged to participate...

(Tom Hills, Devon Wildlife Trust, 1988)

At the last count there were over 100 schools with nurseries and more than 60 community nurseries. In the 6 years the tree bank has been going, 10,000 sapling trees and shrubs have been planted out permanently in coppices, spinneys and hedgerows in 300 different places.

Brede Community Nursery

The nursery started following that hurricane. A landowner in the village offered the use of one of her fields for the village to plant young seedling trees. The county council offered us cut-price trees and we, myself and about 15 other locals, planted 1300 trees in this field including oak, ash, hornbeam, silver birch, wild cherry and chestnut. This was during the course of the winter of 1987/88. In the summer of 1988 the trees flourished. Money to pay for the trees was collected in the village - we had more than enough...In the autumn we offered the trees back to parishioners, free of charge. Some came and dug them up for themselves and for 3 days myself and the volunteers went round planting trees where appropriate...

(Mrs. Marian Mason, Parish Tree Warden, Brede, East Sussex, January 1989).

walnut

Further reading

Avon County Council, Growing Trees from Seed
Devon Wildlife Trust, Devon Tree Bank leaflet, from 35 New Bridge Street, Exeter, Devon, EX4 3AH
Karl Leibscher, 1979, Tree Nurseries, BTCV
M. Yoxon et al, 1977, Ecological Studies in Milton Keynes, (includes section on the collection and storage of tree and shrub seeds.)

COMMUNITY WOODS AND ORCHARDS

There are a large number of small woods and copses throughout the country, many of which are little cared for and largely unused. These are a great potential asset to many local communities. A woodland cared for and/or owned by local people has much to offer
- it is an opportunity to learn about how woods work
- it can be an exciting place in which to walk, rest, play, exercise and observe nature
- it provides a focus for community activity
- it can be a source of wood products for local use - from bean poles and fencing posts for gardeners and farmers, to clothes props and pegs for householders.

- as a source of food - nuts, berries, fruit and mushrooms
- it can ensure a wood is protected from threatened changes. The best way to ensure the survival of small woods is to use and actively care for them involving many people.

Find out about the woods in your locality - who owns them, whether they are used, what for. Much can be discovered by talking to old local people and contacting the council planning department. Use public footpaths to find out more about the woods. If there aren't any appropriate woods in your locality look for a place where you might be able to establish a new wood. If you know of privately owned woods which appear unused you might approach the owner to find out if they might be prepared to sell or lease it to the local community. If a wood is owned by the council find out if they have any plans for it. The council planning department might be able to advise you about suitable areas of existing woodland or land that could be allowed to become woodland.

Some councils are already involved in interesting projects with local woods. In Rochford, Essex, craftsman Jim Partridge is working in Hockley Woods and Thundersley Glen, both owned by the local councils on a project set up jointly with Common Ground and Eastern Arts. Jim has been asked specifically -

to work with Rochford District Council in the design and creation of prototypes for functional items which might be produced and sold by the Council's Woodland Staff
- to respond to particular characteristics of the woods of south east Essex by creating functional artefacts (seats, fences, gates, bridges) which might become local landmarks.

It may help you in your search to find a suitable woodland to form a small group of local people to develop proposals and rally support - possibly making links with established groups such as local amenity groups, and parish or community councils. A leaflet or newsletter, distributed and displayed from the local library, might help you to raise funds to buy land. Your local council will be able to provide advice on sources of grant for land purchase, and might even provide a grant from its own resources.

In A Nutshell

Once you have established your community wood initial work might include making fencing secure to exclude grazing stock and thus encourage natural regeneration and the establishment of saplings; you might also need to thin and harvest some wood and establish paths and routes through the wood. Local fundraising - raffles, subscription and money raised through sale of products from the wood could help cover costs of fencing, tools etc. Grants are available from the Forestry Commission, Countryside Commission and NCC for planting. BTCV/UK2000 and Shell Better Britain sometimes provide small grants for tools. County naturalists' trusts and local Nature Conservancy Council officers, in addition to tree and conservation officers within county or district councils might be able to offer general advice and information about caring for a wood and achieving your objectives.

A number of community woods already exist. In 1981 the Woodland Trust launched a community woodland project, beginning with Pepper Wood, Bromsgrove, and now has 4 community woods in all and a community woodlands officer. They have produced a useful resource pack with suggestions about how to establish a voluntary group; organise practical care and the selling of produce. In Wales, Coed Cymru Woodland Officers with County Councils are giving advice to a number of local councils on how they can care for their own woods.

Bilston Conservation Association, near Wolverhampton, was set up about 10 years ago by local people to save a wood from being destoyed by proposed new development. The community group now look over and care for Peasecroft Wood about 8 acres of woodland dominated by sycamore which developed about 100 years ago on a former colliery tip owned by the local council. The wood is close to the town of Wolverhampton and is well used by local people who hold monthly meetings and do most of the essential practical work, sometimes taking advice from the landscape officer at the borough council.

In Lustleigh, Devon, local people enjoy their town orchard - owned and looked after by the parish council as an informal park. The orchard earns money for the parish from the sale of the apple crop, and even mistletoe and letting grass for sheep grazing. It is also the focus for community festivities - especially during the traditional May Day celebrations and the annual crowning of the May Queen.

In Scotland, a small group of people formed a steering committee, **Borders Community Woodlands**, after hearing of a local wood coming up for sale. With the help of a grant from the Countryside Commission for Scotland, the group purchased the wood in 1987 after a few months of intensive activity - organising local meetings, producing posters and leaflets and attracting much local publicity.

The community woods at Wooplaw will be for the benefit of the local community. A place to walk, play, picnic, study, contemplate and work..... As we are a community based group and not an outside organisation, our strength lies in local involvement, and the multitude of skills and interests which reside within the community.

Basic principles for looking after the wood have been outlined,

- some trees will be allowed to grow on into perpetuity;
- there will be an emphasis on broadleaved species native to the area;
- natural regeneration of desirable species will be encouraged;
- as wide a range as possible of woodland products - timber, poles, firewood, bark, foliage, nuts, berries and fungi will be used locally.
- most trees will be harvested as thinnings and mature timber to enable other trees to be planted.

Borders Community Woodlands has flourished since buying Wooplaw. It now has over 300 members from the local area and produces a regular and informative newsletter.

Further reading

The Woodland Trust, 1986, Community Woodland Resource Pack
Tree Council leaflet, Tree Planting and Community Woodland
Angela King and Sue Clifford, 1987, Holding Your Ground - an action guide to local conservation, Wildwood House
Borders Community Woodlands, Newsletter, send s.a.e. to The Steading, Blainslie, Galashields, TD1 2PR

In A Nutshell

PAPER RECYCLING

We currently recycle less than a third of the paper we use in this country. Each of us consumes about two trees' worth of paper products each year. Newspapers, packaging, envelopes, writing and lavatory papers are all produced mainly with softwood (from conifers). The daily circulation of just one popular newspaper consumes 4000 trees alone.

Nevertheless an increasing number of products are being made from waste paper. It is already the most important indigenous raw material in the British paper making industry. Most of it is used for making packaging and board materials but increasing proportions are being used in the production of newsprint, personal stationery and loo/tissue papers. By using more of these products you not only save trees and help the national paper making industry but you can also:

- reduce the need for costly, disruptive and dangerous landfill sites for municipal waste
- help our balace of payments by cutting the import of paper products and raw materials from other countries
- save energy - making paper from trees uses much more energy than if waste paper is used
- reduce the need for large scale, insensitive and polluting conifer plantations in inappropriate places
- make money.

Less than half the amount of waste paper considered available for recycling is at present used and around half of this is from domestic waste. You can help increase the use of waste paper by organising local collections.

First of all you should find out what schemes may already exist in the locality. Contact the county or borough council, it is the official waste disposal authority - find out if there is a recycling officer, ask if they know of any paper recycling schemes in the area.

Consider how to generate interest among local households and businesses, and find out how local waste paper merchants operate. Here are some starting points:

- look at the level of supply of waste you can expect from your selected area. You could produce a leaflet for local distribution explaining your ideas and asking for help and cooperation. Talk with parish councils and residents/tenants associations. Gather together a group of volunteers.

- discuss your ideas with local waste paper merchants. Find out if they collect waste paper and on what basis - the prices they pay and how these might change. What quantities they are prepared to collect. Can they provide skips? Get an agreement on paper regarding quantities, prices and other arrangements.

- organise regular and efficient collection services. This might simply mean arranging for a skip to be present in an accessible place, for example in a public car park, on a monthly basis. This arrangement would be better for dispersed rural areas. You might need a vehicle to organise door-to-door collections. Advertise in local newspapers and radio.

- you need to encourage people to separate paper from other domestic waste in their homes. In addition by separating newspapers, from magazines, card and other kinds of paper you will get a higher price from the merchants.

- find a safe, secure, fire proof place to store paper, for example a disused garage, a public car park. You should also consider insurance.

Waste Watch, a national campaign set up to encourage better use of resources, have produced a useful information pack called 'Recycling - a practical guide for local groups' which contains some useful advice for groups wishing to start a waste recycling project.

District or county councils should be able to offer initial help and guidance. They might be able to provide some form of sponsorship - or free space for storage. In the 1970's a number of collection schemes stopped because of a sharp drop in prices paid for waste paper. Your local council might be even be able to help by guaranteeing prices for your waste. Further support might come from the Department of the Environment through their Urban Programme, administered by local councils. Small grants, up to £500, are available from the Shell Better Britain Campaign or Waste Watch.

There are already a number of successful waste paper collection schemes organised by local groups around the country. Some make quite large sums of money. Resourcesaver Ltd, in Avon, set up by the local Friends of the Earth group uses a horse and cart for door-to-door collections! In 1984 the group were making around £2000 per month and it was estimated that they were saving ratepayers about £4000 each year. In 1977 Leeds City Council set up Save Waste and Prosper - a scheme to encourage greater recycling of all kind of waste, cans, materials, glass and paper. A network of collection centres, near supermarkets or shopping centres, collected over 2000 tonnes of waste paper in 1985/6, which was a significant contribution to the £30,000 raised from the recycling of all waste for local charities.

Further reading

Waste Watch, 1988, Recycling - a practical giude for local groups, NCVO
FoE, 1989, Once is not Enough
Resource - a monthly magazine published by Avon FoE, Avon Environmental Centre, Junction Road, Brislington, Bristol BS4 3JP
Jo Gordon, 1987, Waste Recycling in the Community, NCVO

In A Nutshell

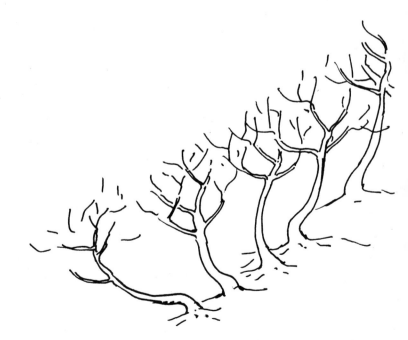

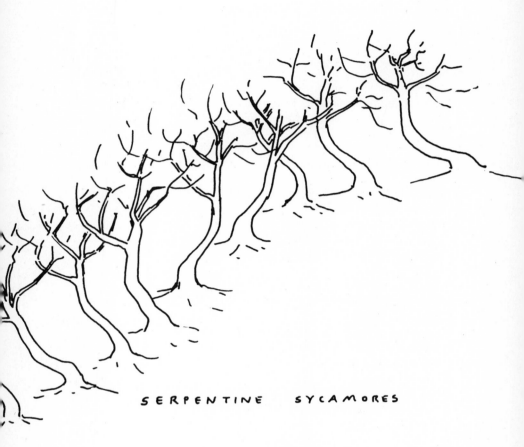

SERPENTINE SYCAMORES

Chapter 4 - **TREE PROTECTION AND THE LAW**

Introduction

Many trees are protected by law from being felled or having branches removed. Individual and small groups of trees and woodlands can be protected by a number of legal provisions. In this section the main provisions are described in summary. Enquiries about specific cases should be addressed to your local tree officer.

There are 5 main ways trees can be protected by law. These are -

- under wild life legislation and civil law
- by Tree Preservation Orders (TPO's)
- in designated Conservation Areas
- by conditions attached to planning permission
- by felling licence control

In addition a number of woodlands identified by the Nature Conservancy Council (NCC) as particularly valuable for wild life are designated National Nature Reserves (NNR's) or Sites of Special Scientific Interest (SSSI's). Many of these are owned by the NCC or voluntary groups such as the RSPB and County Trusts for Nature Conservation, others are cared for under management agreements. A great many trees are covered by more than one form of legal protection.

WILD LIFE LEGISLATION AND CIVIL LAW

Under the 1981 Wildlife and Countryside Act it is illegal to uproot a wild plant unless you are the owner or occupier of the land, or have the owner's permission. Trees are included within the definition of a plant, providing they occur in the wild, that they have not been planted, and are naturally occurring.

Trees are also protected under Civil Law as a form of property. If a tree in your ownership is damaged a prosecution can be made, providing there is a witness. Ealing Borough Council recently successfully prosecuted a drunk who was fined £200 for damaging a street tree.

TREE PRESERVATION ORDERS

TPO's are at present the most effective way of protecting trees from being felled or damaged. Any individual tree, group of trees or woodland can be protected by a TPO under the provisions of the Town and Country Planning Act, 1971. Special consent is however required from the relevant government department if the trees are on Crown Land and local authorities are often reluctant to use TPO's on trees on land in their own ownership.

TPO's can be made by a district, borough or county council. You can find out which trees in your locality are covered by Orders by consulting the TPO register and map which you can find at the district council offices, usually in the planning department.

Anyone can get an Order placed on a tree - you don't have to own it. If you know of a tree that you think should be protected by a TPO write to the local council tree officer with details of where it is, preferably showing the location on a map, and the reasons why you think it should be protected. The council will usually make an Order if they are satisfied the trees benefit the public in some way. They will take into account the following factors in making a decision:

- the trees must normally be visible from a public place - a road, footpath or park
- the benefit may be realised sometime in the future, for example when a new development has been completed
- if the tree is intrinsically beautiful
- if the trees contribute to the landscape
- if they screen an eyesore
- if the trees are locally scarce
- if they are important as a home for wild life.

If the council agrees to make an Order, they will inform the owner, and usually allow 6 weeks for them to appeal, after which the council will make a decision based on any comments received.

If you believe a tree is in imminent danger of being felled contact the council tree officer immediately, saying where the tree is and why you are concerned. If the tree is already covered by a TPO then the tree officer should contact the owner and inform them that this is the case and permission should be sought before a tree is touched. If there is no TPO the tree officer should be able to place an emergency TPO in just a few hours which will be effective for up to 6 months, before being replaced by a full TPO. Find out before an emergency arises if your local tree officer has the delegated powers necessary to issue a TPO at short notice. If they don't, press the chief planning officer for these powers to be made available.

Although what constitutes a tree has not been defined in legislation, TPO's are not normally made on plants with a main stem less than 7 or so inches in diameter. However Order's can apply to the rootstock of a tree providing it is able to regenerate and regrow. Coppice woods and trees can therefore be protected by a TPO, though regular cutting of coppice wood will not usually require permission under an Order. Hedgerow trees can be protected by a TPO although hedges as such are not strictly covered by tree preservation legislation. However if the trees constituting a hedge are over 15 feet high and are not regularly trimmed, a TPO can be made. In Wisbech the district council recently issued a TPO to protect a hedgerow because of concern over local loss of hedgerows due to farming changes.

Roger Deakin describes how Cowpasture Lane, a medieval green lane with an ancient hedgerow and trees, was saved from being converted to farming land through the use of a TPO, even after many of the trees had been cut down.

The owner made two appeals to the DoE against conditions imposed by the local council for the conservation of hedges and trees in Cowpasture Lane. He succeeded in gaining an extra metre width for the access track he was to clear for his machines but failed to persuade the minister to allow him to uproot the whole of the field boudary hedge down one side of the Lane.
The decision on the first appeal (July, 1983) noted that 'there is no bar to the use of TPO's to protect trees in hedges or trees that constitute a hedge, provided that the trees are of reasonable height and have not been regularly trimmed.' And in dismissing the second appeal (March, 1985) it was noted that, 'Vigorous, healthy coppice stools are developing from the tree

stumps...from the available evidence it is clear that the Lane is a wild life corridor and refuge for a range of plants and animals and is enjoyed and appreciated by many people who use the public right-of-way along it. It is further considered that the Lane constitutes an amenity, of which the boundary ditches are, with the adjacent hedges, an integral part, The agricultural benefits to the adjacent field have been fully considered but the view is taken that the removal of the tree stumps would constitute an unnecessary step towards the gradual destruction of this significant landscape feature.'

The Lane is now returning to it's former splendour under the care of the Suffolk Wildlife Trust, who have agreed, in consultation with the counicl and owner, a regular cycle of coppicing and hedgetrimming.

(Roger Deakin, March, 1989)

Until recently local councils used to be wary of placing Orders on woodland for fear of being liable to pay huge sums in compensation due to the loss of value of the land. It 1988, following a well-publicised case involving Canterbury City Council, the law was changed so that as long as an Order is accompanied by a certificate stating that the Order is made in the interests of good forestry or **amenity,** then compensation cannot be claimed. This means that woodlands can now be protected by a TPO simply because of their contribution to the landscape, without councils being financially liable (see Town and Country Planning (Tree Preservation Order) (Amendment) Regulations, 1988, S.I. no. 963).

In A Nutshell

Anyone wanting to lop, top, fell or uproot a tree covered by a TPO must first obtain permission from the local council - usually the district or borough council, though sometimes the county. Exceptions include if planning permission has been awarded (which overrides the TPO); where trees are in an orchard or managed for fruit production; if work is necessary in the work of the statutory authorities; or if work is being carried out in accordance with an Act of Parliament. An owner can fell a tree if it is considered 'dead, dying or dangerous' but, except in an emergency, the owner must first consult the council. If a tree is cut down for this reason the landholder has a duty to plant another tree as soon as possible. There is also a commonlaw right for owners of land to cut back the branches of a tree which overhang their property and are causing a nuisance even if it is protected by a TPO, but it has to be shown that actual damage has been abated by the action.

Where an application is made for work considered to be essential to the future health of the tree it will usually be allowed. If an owner doesn't agree with the decision of a council an appeal can be made to the Secretary of State for the Environment. An appointed inspector will then consider the case on the basis of written representations and sometimes a visit to the trees in question.

The council can prosecute any person they suspect has contravened a TPO. If convicted they will be liable to a fine of up to £2000 and an order to replant with another tree. It is not a defence for an owner or contractor to say they didn't know about the TPO, Orders are registered in the local Land Charges Register and the existence of a TPO should be revealed in a solicitors' search and will be included in conveyancing documents relating to a property.

Tree Preservation Orders can be easily ignored by unscrupulous owners. Tree officers are not in a position to keep a close eye on all the protected trees in their area. They rely heavily on local people to let them know if any trees are under threat. Be vigilant and contact your local tree officer immediately if you suspect something's afoot - be alert for crosses on trees, the sound of chainsaws and piles of logs.

CONSERVATION AREAS

In places designated as 'Conservation Areas' (under the Town and Country Amenities Act, 1974) trees are afforded added protection. Anyone wishing to do work on a tree is required to give the local council 6 weeks notice in writing before carrying out the work. There are 5,000 Conservation Areas in Britain. They are designated by district councils to preserve the character of areas 'of special architectural or historic interest'. Conservation Areas cover buildings, streets, town centres and occasionally landscapes of historic interest - you can find out if there is one in your locality by contacting the local council's planning department.

Many people do not know that they live in a Conservation Area. If you live in one make sure that your neighbours, residents and tenants associations and parish councils know. You could prepare a leaflet for local distribution outlining the special protection afforded trees in the area.

PLANNING CONDITIONS

When planning permission is given for a new development which will affect trees protected by a TPO, the Order is usually rendered ineffective. However conditions attached to a planning permission, which lay out rules that developers must obey, can ensure that certain trees are retained and new ones are planted.

Guidelines for the protection of trees on development sites are often also issued to developers by district or county councils if planning permission is granted. Make sure that they place emphasis on tree retention and planting when detailing planning permission. Here are excerpts from conditions relating to trees used by a London Borough Council.

Details of all existing trees on site with a stem diameter of 100mm or greater shall be supplied to the Council prior to the consideration of detailed proposals...Where nearby excavations are proposed, the level at the base of each tree shall be included. Trees to be removed in conjunction with the proposed development should be indicated as such and, where appropriate, the proposed positions and lines of protective fencing and prohibited areas should be shown...

All trees on the site, unless shown on the permitted drawings as being removed, shall be retained and protected to the satisfaction of the Council... By not later than the end of the planting season following the completion of the development...trees shall be planted on the land in such positions and of such size and species as may be agreed with the Council. Any tree removed, dying, being severely damaged or becoming seriously diseased within 5 years of planting shall be replaced by trees of a similar size and species...

Find out what guidelines your council issues for tree protection during development work and ensure that these are observed and planning conditions enforced. If particularly valuable trees are threatened by a new development ask the council to enter into a Section 52 agreement (under the 1971 Town and Country Planning Act) to protect them. This is a stronger measure than a planning condition and it can be legally binding.

FELLING LICENCES

In addition to tree protection exercised by district and county councils, the Forestry Commission (FC) operate a system of control over tree felling. Very little felling can be done without a felling licence.

A felling licence is required where it is proposed to fell trees eqiuvalent to more than 5 cubic metres in volume in a 3 month period - equivalent to about 3 large trees. (If less than 5 cubic metres are to be felled, but more than 2 cubic metres are to be sold then a licence is still required).

Trees may be protected by other legislation but a **felling licence** is not required if trees are:

- in a garden, orchard, churchyard or public open space, for example a park;
- interfering with permitted development or statutory works by public bodies;
- if below 8 cm in diameter measured 1.3 m above ground (8cm '

diameter breast height'. 10cm for thinnings, 15cm for coppice);
- if felling is in accordance with a plan set out under the FC's
  Woodland Grant Scheme;
- if felling complies with an Act of Parliament.

If someone is felling a number of trees in your locality you can find out if a felling licence has been issued by contacting the Forestry Commission District Office. If you think the felling is being carried out illegally, alert them. Owners carrying out illegal felling can be fined up to £1000 or twice the value of the trees whichever is the higher. They can also be made to restock the land and maintain the trees for 10 years.

When a felling licence is required the owner must apply to the Forestry Commission. The trees will then be inspected by an officer from one of the FC's local offices (address in telephone book) who will sometimes consult with interested bodies, including the district

and/or county council, and the Nature Conservancy Council if in an SSSI or National Nature Reserve. If the trees are also covered by a TPO, the Commission will pass on the application to the county or district council for consideration as a TPO application.

Although the consultation procedure has improved in recent years, it is still very much up to the FC to choose who to consult and there is no guarantee the views of consultees will be given any weight. A district council consulted by the Forestry Commission over felling licence applications can itself choose to make information available for inspection by local people. Find out if your district council publicises lists of applications - some send details to parish councils or county trusts for nature conservation for comment. If they don't, ask them to keep you informed. If you don't agree with any felling that is being proposed, let the council know - write to the tree or forestry officer and inform your local councillors and MP. Permission to fell is usually accompanied by a requirement to replant with broadleaved trees. If this isn't complied with then owners can be fined.

Disputed cases are referred to one of seven Regional Advisory Committees (RAC) who are required to advertise details. Previously dominated by timber interests, the committees have recently been required to include representatives of nature conservation, recreation and landscape interests. You can find out who sits on your RAC by contacting the local FC office. If you don't agree with an application you are entitled to object in writing to the RAC who then make recommendations to the Forestry Commissioners who are the final arbiters.

Where felling of woods owned by the Forestry Commission is proposed the Commission is required to consult county and/or district councils. Again in disputed cases you are entitled to make representations to the Regional Advisory Committee, to be taken into account when making their recommendations.

Further reading

Department of the Environment (DoE), 1988, Protected Trees - a guide to tree preservation (available from DoE, Tollgate House,

Houlton Street, Bristol BS2 9DJ or your district or county council)
Woodland Trust, 1987, Trees, the Law and You
FoE, 1988, Briefing Sheet on TPO's
DoE Cicular 36/78 - Trees and Forestry, (out of print).
Forestry Commission booklets - Control of Tree Felling, 1987 and
Consultation Procedures, 1984. Both available from FC, Edinburgh
or local offices.
NCC, Wildlife, the Law and You
Angela King and S.ue Clifford, 1987, Holding Your Ground - an
action guide to local conservation, Wildwood House.

Chapter 5 - **ORGANISATIONS CONCERNED WITH TREES**

This section provides a brief introduction to the main organisations concerned with trees in Britain. It has a number of purposes - to help you identify who is responsible for particular trees and woods and the decisions affecting them; to describe the role of government and non-government organisations with relation to trees; and to outline the sources of advice and support for protecting and caring for trees. If you are seeking financial support for a project involving trees you should read this chapter in conjunction with the following one.

LOCAL GOVERNMENT

Outside the main conurbations elected local government is currently divided into 3 levels - parish councils (also known as town or community councils), district councils (sometimes called borough or city councils) and county councils. In the main conurbations there is now only one level of local government, the district (borough or city council). Each level has a responsibility for trees.

Parish and Community Councils - cover all of the rural areas in England, Wales and Scotland. In some small towns they are called town councils. Potentially these local councils have a great deal of power. They are usually consulted by the district council about proposals for new building and development (planning applications), on the preparation of local and county plans, and on major

hedge - ash and sycamore.

work proposed by statutory undertakers - such as the water author-ites, gas or electicity boards. (Although statutory undertakers are exempted from many of the provisions of existing tree protection and this anomaly is likely to become an increasing problem as more of these services are performed by private companies). They are also consulted by the district council on applications for work on trees protected by a TPO or in a Conservation Area and sometimes Felling Licence applications.

Many parish councils own and look after land, such as local parks, allotments and other open areas. In some instances, where Parochial Church Councils (which are the church bodies quite separate from civil parish councils) have relinquished control, they may also care for churchyards and cemeteries.

If you live in an area with a parish or community council, find out what it does and who the councillors are. You should find minutes of meetings and the address of the parish or community council clerk, who will be able to tell you the names of the councillors and more about council affairs, in the local library. Why not become a councillor yourself?

District and Borough Councils - The district council (known as the borough or city council in some urban areas) is the official Local Planning Authority for your area. The planning department of the district receive most applications for planning permission for devel

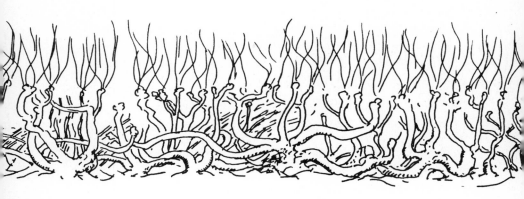

opment and consider whether permission should be given or refused, and any conditions that should be imposed. Planning officers make recommendations to the planning committee which comprises elected local councillors. The planning department is also responsible for administering TPO's and controlling work on trees in designated Conservation Areas.

If you want to find out which trees have TPO's on them, or propose new ones, you should contact the tree officer and ask if you can see the register of Tree Preservation Orders. A tree officer or tree preservation officer, usually attached to the planning department (s/he might sometimes be a landscape architect, countryside officer or a planning officer with responsibility for trees), makes recommendations to the planning committee on enforcing TPO and Conservation Area legislation and placing new Orders. Except in particularly contentious cases, they frequently have delegated powers from the planning committee to take their own decisions on these matters.

A tree officer is usually only responsible for trees on privately owned land. Trees on council owned land, such as those in parks, streets and on roadsides and in housing estates, are usually the responsibility of an arboriculture officer in the parks and recreation or leisure department. The arboriculture officer and team will carry out such work as annual trimming and pruning and tree planting on council owned land. If you are concerned about the health of a tree or know of damaged trees in your street, housing estate or local park - or want a tree planted - contact the arboriculture officer.

The work of other departments will have a bearing on trees. For example Environmental Health Departments are responsible for monitoring air pollution near roads and from industrial and domestic sources. Find out if the parks and planning departments use this information in deciding where to plant and protect trees? Encourage them to do so.

District councils are also responsible for domestic waste collection. Some have appointed recycling officers and developed recycling schemes, including waste paper collection. Find out if your council encourages recycling.

County Councils cover most of England and Wales outside the major conurbations. They are the Highways Authority - responsible for main roads and tree planting on roadside locations (excluding motorways and trunk roads); and the Waste Authority - responsible for preparing waste disposal plans and controlling waste disposal sites. They are also a planning authority responsible for deciding planning applications likely to have an impact wider than the district level, for example mineral extraction. County councils are consulted by statutory undertakers and the MAFF concerning proposed major work, such as extensive land drainage and underground services.

The planning department of the county council usually has a countryside section which deals with issues relating to trees and woods in the county. After the district council tree officer, you should contact the countryside section if you have an enquiry about tree protection. A forestry officer, usually attached to this section will be able to give advice on economic aspects of woodland management and contentious felling proposals. They will also be able to tell you about availability of grant aid. (If you live in one of the ten designated National Parks in England and Wales, the separate National Parks Authority will have its own trees and woodland officer.)

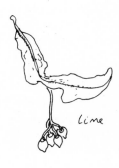

Lime

In A Nutshell

NATIONAL AGENCIES

There are 3 main national agencies whose area of responsibility encompasses trees and woods - the Nature Conservancy Council; Countryside Commissions and Forestry Commission. All three agencies receive major funding from government and are both agents for putting into practice government policy and advisers to government on specific topics. There is some conflict between these organisations where their roles overlap and they impinge on each others' responsibilities.

The Nature Conservancy Council

(Headquarters, Northminster House, Northminster Road, Peterborough, PE1 1UA; NCC (Wales) Plas Penrhos, Penrhos Road, Bangor, Gwynedd LL57 2LQ; NCC (Scotland) 12 Hope Terrace, Edinburgh, EH9 2AS)

The NCC was established in 1973 'for the purposes of nature conservation and fostering the understanding thereof'. It is the main scientific advisory body to government on such matters. It's work ranges from the protection of key habitats and sites, and certain species of plants and animals; to conducting and commissioning research, and the provision of advice, information and grant aid to local authorities, voluntary organisations, schools and other groups. The NCC is divided into fifteen regional offices which can provide information and advice about nature reserves and SSSI's in the locality (addresses in telephone directory or from HQ in Peterborough).

The NCC owns, leases or manages over 230 sites, prime examples of Britain's wild life and geological features, as National Nature Reserves and establishes management agreements and notifies owners of potentially damaging operations on a large number of SSSI's. It has compiled a county-based inventory of ancient woodland. The NCC gives grants to other organisations, such as the RSPB, the National Trust and Woodland Trust, for land purchase. It is getting increasingly involved in partnerships and community activities.

It has a mail order catalogue which lists research reports, teachers' material, posters, wallcharts and booklets, such as 'Why Plant Native Broadleaf Trees' - obtainable from Peterborough.

Countryside Commissions

(Headquarters (England and Wales), John Dower House, Crescent Place, Cheltenham, Glos., GL50 3RA; publications, PO Box 7, Manchester, M19 2M; (Scotland) Battleby, Redgerton, Perth PH1 3EW)

The Countryside Commissions are the government's advisers on landscape conservation and access and recreation. The Commissions cover the whole countryside and have overall responsibility for National Parks (in England and Wales) and Areas of Outstanding Natural Beauty, Country Parks and long distance paths. They provide advice and finance for the conservation of natural beauty and the 'provision and improvement of facilities for the enjoyment

of the countryside and access for open-air recreation'. The English Commission , based in Cheltenham, has eight regional offices, each of which can provide practical advice, and information on policy and grant-aid. Regional offices frequently work closely with county and district councils and voluntary organisations.

The Countryside Commissions' remits do not include pollution matters even though what they are trying to conserve can be destroyed by acid rain and other forms of pollution.

A special unit Task Force Trees was set up by the Countryside Commission in the south east of England to provide advice and funds after the storm in October, 1987. An excellent Action Pack has been produced - more information from Publications Dept. in Manchester

The Countryside Commission (England and Wales) has recently launched an Urban Forest initiative in the North East and east of London and a major new forest in the Midlands. A policy statement produced in 1987, 'Forestry in the Countryside' argues that "national forestry policy should be based on multiple objectives. These should be to:
- produce a national supply of timber as a raw material and as a source of energy;
- offer an alternative to agricultural use of land;
- contribute to rural employment, either in timber industries or through associated recreation developments;
- create attractive sites for public enjoyment;
- enhance the natural beauty of the countryside;
- create wildlife habitats."

Forestry Commission

(Headquarters, 231 Costorphine Road, Edinburgh, EH12 7AT; Publications, Forest Research Station, Alice Holt Lodge, Wrecclesham, Farnham, Surrey, GU10 4LH)

The Forestry Commission was set up in 1919 with the aim of creating new forests. Its principal objective is the "efficient production of wood for industry." It has a dual role of establishing and managing its own forests, the Forestry Enterprise, and providing advice, encouragement and grants to other bodies, the Forestry Authority. It's role includes 'the collection and dissemination of forestry information; the development of education and training in forestry; the conduct of forestry research....the provision of advice and financial aid to private forestry...the regulation of felling and the control of

tree pests and diseases.' The Forestry Commission produces research notes, bulletins and leaflets on a range of different topics including forest management, disease control and fencing. A catalogue of publications is available from the Forestry Research Station
in Surrey. Through the Forestry Research Council it organises
forestry skill courses run by approved instructors around the country.

With its HQ in Edinburgh, the Commission is divided into 7 Regional Conservancies covering England, Scotland and Wales. Local
offices deal with felling licence applications and planting proposals.
They have arrangements for consulting district and county councils;
the NCC where designated Nature Reserves and SSSI's are involved
(conflict does occur, see below); and the Countryside Commissions.
The Forestry Commission does not usually consult beyond these
statutory groups. Find out from your district council and local FC
office (see telephone directory) what arrangements there are for
consultation. Contentious cases are referred to Regional Advisory
Committees who make recommendations to the Forestry Commissioners for a decision. Although the Commission are now supposed
to take into account the views of the consulted bodies - many groups
understandibly argue for greater public accountability.

In 1988 the FC owned around 40% of the area of woodland in Britain
- over 90% of which comprises conifers - mainly spruce, pine and
larch. Free public access is allowed in Commission woods. Since
1981 however it has been required by the government to sell-off
plantations and land for planting. Concern has been expressed that
once sold, public access to ex-Forestry Commission will be stopped.

For a number of years there have been worries that the Forestry
Commission has been pursuing its main objective of timber production without proper consideration of the impact of its activities on
the landscape and nature conservation. In 1985 the government
gave the Forestry Commission a duty to achieve a "balance between
the interests of forestry and the environment". Some Commission
forests include National Nature Reserves and SSSI's and conservation plans and management agreements are being drawn up for
these areas.

The forestry industry has a huge planting target of around 33,000 ha each year which includes FC and private sector planting. The Forestry Commission has recently come into conflict with the NCC and other conservation groups over the affects of blanket afforestation in upland areas. Afforestation in many instances reduces the variety of wild life and causes acidification of water resources. The NCC is pressing the Commission to take greater account of wild life and nature conservation factors when deciding planting policy. Conflict has focussed on proposals to plant extensive conifer forests in the Flow Country, an internationally important area of upland bog in the Scottish Highlands. From July, 1988, the FC may require applicants for grant aid for forestry planting to conduct and Environmental Assessment of their plans.

NATIONAL GOVERNMENT

There are two main bodies of national government whose work has a direct impact on trees and woods - the Department of Environment and the Ministry of Agriculture, Fisheries and Food. There are other parts of national government whose work concerns trees indirectly. The **Department of Transport** are responsible for emissions from cars and lorries, which contribute to acid rain and ozone, both damaging to trees. Lobby the Deptartment to control vehicle emissions - press for the mandatory fitting of catalytic converters to all new cars.

In addition the work of the **Pollution Inspectorate** for England and Wales, HM Industrial Pollution Inspectorate of Scotland and the Alkali and Radio Chemical Inspectorate of Northern Ireland, has a bearing on trees through their control of pollution from major industries which are registered with them. They operate a system of pollution consents which are designed to minimise harmful pollution, such as the sulphur dioxide which creates the acid rain which harms trees. In enforcing the consents the Inspectorate has the ability to inspect premises and require improvements, but the role is mainly one of education and gentle persuasion. The Inspectorate is divided into regions and districts which deal with the registered industries in their area. Regional offices can give you information on consents for local industries and action taken on infringements. If you have a complaint about pollution from a local industry contact the district inspector. You'll find the address in the telephone directory - or ask you local environmental health officer.

Department of the Environment

The Department of the Environment (DoE) is responsible for most matters concerning local government and major land use planning issues - such as new international airports and major transport links, and policy on pollution control and waste disposal. Major applications for new development will usually be considered by the DoE. They also approve structure plans and local plans drawn up by county and district councils.

Appeals against district or county council decisions on planning applications and applications to carry out work on trees protected by a TPO are made to the DoE. TPO appeals are usually considered by the DoE Inspectorate in Bristol. These appeals are commonly by written representations, where aggrieved parties submit their cases in writing to the Inspector appointed by the DoE. The Inspector will normally visit the site to assess the case. In 1986 the DoE received 293 such appeals and it was estimated that original decisions were upheld in around half of the cases. Appeals against planning decisions are sometimes considered by a full local inquiry where applicants, concerned local groups and expert witnesses present their cases before an Inspector appointed by the DoE.

The Ministry of Agriculture, Fisheries and Food

MAFF administers the government's agricultural policy in England. The respective organisations in Wales, Scotland and Northern Ireland are the Welsh Office of Agricultural Development; the Dept of Agriculture and Forestry in Scotland; and the Dept of Agriculture Northern Ireland. The government's policy is strongly influenced by the Common Agricultural Policy of the EEC. For a handbook about MAFF's work, 'At the Farmer's Service', and information about other publications write to MAFF/Publications, Lion House, Willowburn Estate, Alnwick, Northumberland, NE66 2PF.

The Agriculture and Development Advisory Service (ADAS) is the part of the Ministry in regular contact with farmers, providing advice on animal health, technical information, and grant aid. Contact your local ADAS office (address in telephone directory under Agriculture Fisheries and Food) for further information about the services it offers and costs. In Scotland the Colleges of Agriculture perform this function.

Many of the grant schemes administered by the MAFF have caused major changes in farming throughout Britain. For the past 40 years the emphasis has been on increased food production, often at the expense of conservation and other demands on the countryside. More recently food surpluses have brought about a major shift in objectives and emphasis is now put on finding alternative uses of farmland, including woodland. At the moment there are 3 main schemes with a bearing on trees and woods - Set- aside - a scheme designed to cut surpluses of arable production by paying farmers to take 20% of their arable land out of production for 5 years and either leave fallow or convert to woodland; the Farm Woodland Scheme - which aims to encourage farmers to plant new woodland on arable land and improved grassland through annual payments (linked with the Forestry Commission schemes) and the recently announced Farm and Conservation Grants Scheme. Grants available under each scheme are discussed in the following chapter. The Ministry have also produced information packs on the schemes which are available from local ADAS offices.

In addition to these schemes, in designated Environmentally Sensitive Areas (ESA's) there is special advice and payments available to farmers who agree to farm in a manner beneficial to conservation. There are 18 ESA's in Britain, including parts of the South Downs, Pennine Dales, the Broads, and Shropshire Borders. Although arrangements vary from place to place, payments may cover woodland management, care of old orchards, hedge retention and control of chemical use. In the Somerset Levels for example, farmers enter agreements to pollard willows on a 5-7 year cycle. County Councils may also be able to provide information on ESA schemes in their areas - contact the countryside section or Farming Conservation (FWAG) Adviser.

VOLUNTARY ORGANISATIONS

There are numerous voluntary organisations and charities concerned with trees and woods. We list here some of the national groups, divided between landholders and those without land, with a brief description of their roles. Many of the groups have a membership and publish leaflets, reports, newsletters or magazines - write to them for further information - always help with a stamped addressed envelope. For timber growers there are many professional associations concerned with forestry, such as the Royal Forestry Society and Timber Growers (U.K.) - addresses can be obtained from the Forestry Commission.

Voluntary Organisations - **Landholders**

The Woodland Trust, Autumn Park, Dysart Road, Grantham, Lincs, NG31 6LL (0486 74297) - A national charity concerned with protecting trees and woods by purchasing them. It owns and cares for more than 350 woods, covering over 11,000 acres, which are open for all to enjoy, throughout England, Wales and Scotland. It also operates a Licence Scheme (currently being revised) whereby the Trust helps landholders to create new woodland when for one reason or another they can't undertake the planting or maintenance themselves. After 25 years the licence expires and the trees become the property of the owner, who will be expected to contribute to costs of fencing. Write to the Trust for further details of the Scheme and properties they own.

The National Trust, 36 Queen Anne's Gate, London, SW1H 9AS (01-222-9251) **National Trust for Scotland**, 5 Charlotte Square, Edinburgh EH2 4DU (031 226 5922) - One of the oldest environmental groups in Britain, established in 1895 to purchase land and buildings to protect them from development 'for the benefit of the nation'. It owns around half a million acres of land covering National Nature Reserves and SSSI's, and including large areas of woodland, as well as over 290 houses and gardens.

Royal Society for the Protection of Birds, The Lodge, Sandy, Beds, SG19 2DL (0767-80551) - Set up in 1889 to conserve wild birds and their habitats. It has a membership and manages 114 nature reserves

- including many woods - covering 180,000 acres, to which members have free access. The RSPB Conservation Management Advisory Service provide advice and information on aspects of woodland management for birds and have produced research reports and leaflets, such as 'New Farm Woods For Birds' to encourage land-holders to make woods more attractive for birds and other wild life.

Royal Society for Nature Conservation, The Green, Nettleham, Lincoln, LN2 2NR (0522 752326) - The national group representing the 48 County Trusts for Nature Conservation. Each Trust promotes conservation of nature and wild life in its area by purchasing and managing reserves, education and liaison with landholders, local government and Statutory Undertakers. Trusts own or manage 1,684 reserves. The RSNC junior organisation WATCH is currently involved in a project involving walnut trees.

Voluntary Organisations - **Non-Landholders**

The Arboricultural Association, Ampfield House, Romsey, Hants. SO5 9PA (0794 68717) - Represents the interests of people involved in caring for trees as a profession - local authority arboriculture officers, tree consultants and contractors. It provides technical information and produces a 'Directory of Registered Arboricultural Consultants and Approved Tree Contractors'.

British Trust for Conservation Volunteers, (BTCV), 36 St. Mary's St, Wallingford, Oxon, OX10 0EU (0491-39766) - Concerned with practical conservation tasks - promoting and organising voluntary work around the country - including dry stone walling, restoration of footpaths and work in woodlands. Through 11 regional offices and 460 local groups, BTCV provides transport, training courses, tools and other equipment for practical tasks.

CLEAR (Campaign for Lead Free Air), 3 Endsleigh Street, London, WC1H 0DD (01-278-9686) - Promotes the use of unleaded petrol to reduce environmental lead pollution. It runs an unleaded petrol information line and has produced guides to which cars will run on unleaded petrol and where it can be obtained.

Civic Trust, 17 Carlton House Terrace, London SW1Y 5AW (01-930-

0914) - Encourages the protection and improvement of the built environment. It comprises four independent associate Trusts in the NE, NW, Scotland and Wales. Over 1,000 local amenity societies are registered with the Trust which promotes their concerns nationally and provides advice.

Coed Cymru, Ladywell House, Frolic Street, Newtown, Powys, SY16 1RD (0686-28514) - Set up to encourage the use and protection of the native woods of Wales. The steering group consists of representatives of the Countryside and Forestry Commissions, the NCC and Welsh Office Agriculture Department. There is a Coed Cymru Officer in each of the Welsh county councils and National Parks who provides free advice on woodland management and grant aid to farmers and landholders and promotes community woods.

Common Ground, 45 Shelton Street, London WC2H 9HJ (01-379-3109) - The Trees, Woods and Green Man project is intended to heighten awareness of trees and woods by stressing the importance of their aesthetic, spiritual and cultural value as well as ecological importance. It is doing this through all branches of the arts - exhibitions and publications as well as practical guides to tree care in town and country. Common Ground also has a campaign to Save Old Orchards and Plant New Ones (leaflet available on receipt of sae).

Council for the Protection of Rural England, 4 Hobart Place, London, SW1W 0HY (01-235-9481); **Council for the Protection of Rural Wales**, Ty Gwyn, 31 High St, Welshpool, Powys, SY21 7PJ (0938-2525); **Association for the Protection of Rural Scotland**, 1 Thistle Court, Edinburgh 2 (031 225 6744) - Concerned to protect the countryside - including woodland - from threats from new development, roads, mines, power stations and changing farming practices. CPRE has a network of 44 county branches and local groups who often organise their own campaigns. It monitors government policy on countryside conservation and has been outspoken in its criticism of recent forestry policy.

The Farming and Wildlife Trust, National Agricultural Centre, Stoneleigh, Kenilworth, Warwickshire CV8 2LZ (0203-696699) - Set up by farmers and conservationists to seek ways of reconciling agriculture with wildlife and landscape conservation. Many counties have Farming and Wildlife Advisory Groups and Farm Conservation Advisers who can provide advice to farmers on farm woodlands. Contact your county council or local ADAS office to find out the address of your local Adviser.

Friends of the Earth, 26-28 Underwood Street, London N1 7JQ (01-490-1555) - Part of an international network and organises campaigns, conferences and commissions research on a range of issues - from air pollution and waste disposal to tropical rain forests and Cities for People. It has a network of more than 230 local groups who lobby MP's, local councils and businesses, set up recycling schemes, organise talks, demonstrations and exhibitions. In 1988 they took part in Forest Alert - a project to survey and draw attention to pollution damage to trees. It has produced the 'Good Wood Guide' to businesses who only use and sell wood from sustainable sources. It has produced a number of reports on acid rain and a TPO Briefing Sheet. (Friends of the Earth Scotland, 53 George 1V Bridge, Edinburgh, EH1 1EJ (031-225-6906), is campaigning against acid rain and afforestation).

Greenpeace Environmental Trust, 30-31 Islington Green, London, N1 8XE
(01-354-5100) - Part of an international group which organises campaigns and direct action on a range of environmental problems - including whaling, acid rain and water pollution. It has commissioned research on air pollution damage to Briatin's trees and has produced a number of reports, including 'Acid Rain - it's happening here' by Chris Rose and 'Tree Survey of Southern England' by Andrew Tickle, both for Greenpeace, 1988.

The Greenwood Trust, Rose Cottage, Dale Road, Coalbrookdale, Telford, Shropshire, TF8 7DS (095245 3080) - Founded in 1984 to promote "the educational and commercial value of small woodlands." It promotes coppicing at it's educational centre at Telford and organises regular demonstrations, lectures and other educational activities.

The Men of the Trees, Crawley Down, Crawley, Sussex, RH10 4HL (0342 712536) - An international organisation dedicated to the planting and protection of trees. Founded in 1912 by Richard St. Barbe Baker in Africa, it has 18 county branches in Britain which organise walks, talks, tree planting and related local activities.

National Association of Local Councils, 108 Gt. Russell St, London, WC1B 3LD (01-637-1865) - The umbrella body for parish and community councils.

National Council for Voluntary Organisations, 26 Bedford Square, London WC1B 3HU (01-636-4066) - Runs 'Waste Watch', a national initiative to promote recycling.

The National Society for Clean Air, 136 North Street, Brighton, BN1 1RG (0273 26313) - Campaigns for the prevention of air pollution, from noise to acid rain and lead pollution. Has 12 regional divisions in the UK which hold meetings to discuss local issues. The Society organises an annual conference and training workshops on technical matters and makes representations to government and industry on legislation, pollution standards and local issues. It has produced a series of useful leaflets on acid rain, lead pollution and garden bonfires with advice on how to prevent pollution.

The Open Spaces Society, 25A Bell Street, Henley-on-Thames, Oxon, RG9 2BA (0491 573535) - Fights to protect common land, village greens, open spaces and public paths by giving advice to local councils and communities.

The Ramblers Association, 1-5 Wandsworth Road, London, SW8 2XX
(01-582-6878)- Aims to promote rambling and access to open country, protect rights of way and the countryside. Local groups organise regular walks, and in 1988 the Association organised a conference on Forests for Recreation.

The Royal Horticultural Society, 80 Vincent Square, London, SW1 (01-834-4333); RHS Garden and Fruit Identification at Wisley, Woking, Surrey, GU23 6QB (0483 224234) - Concerned with trees in gardens. It has a number of model gardens of different sizes at its own garden at Wisley. It also has a large orchard with over 500 different varieties of apples and can supply bud or graft wood for any of them. The Society also have a Fruit Identification Service where a range of tree fruits can be identified for a small charge.

Scottish Community Woods Campaign, 3 Kenmore Street, Aberfeldy, Perthshire, PH15 2AW (0887 20392) - Aims to 'promote the expansion and sustainable use of native woodland in the context of the development and support of the Local Community Woodlands Intiative throughout Scotland'. The Campaign promotes the 'Growing Up with Trees' project with primary schools, encouraging seed collection and the establishment of tree nurseries using Scottish native trees.

The Tree Council, 35 Belgrave Square, London, SW1X 8QN (01-235-8854) - A national umbrella organisation of groups involved with trees, formed in 1974 to "improve the environment in town and country by promoting the planting and good maintenance of suitable trees; to disseminate knowledge about trees and their care; to act as a forum for organisation concerned with trees, to identify national problems and to provide initiatives for cooperation." It does not get involved in practical projects itself but coordinates National Tree Week in November each year. It has produced leaflets on planting trees and doing a tree survey.

UK2000, Butler's Wharf Business Centre, 45 Curlew Street, London SE1 2ND - A national environmental improvement campaign which coordinates the work of voluntary organisations and provides grant-aid for local community environmental projects. UK2000 is coordinating the establishment of a National Small Woodlands Association promoting the effective use of small woods.

The World Wide Fund for Nature - UK, Panda House, Weyside Park, Godalming, Surrey GU7 1XR (0483-426444) - Part of an international organisation which fund raises and campaigns on a range of issues affecting wild life and trees, including air pollution and rainforest destruction.

Chapter 6 - **SOURCES OF GRANT AID**

Introduction

The preceding chapters show that there is much you can do to care for trees without the need for large sums of money. There is no need to buy trees for planting - you can grow them yourself at little or no cost; it doesn't cost anything to ensure that existing trees are given the protection that is afforded them by current legislation. Lobbying to ensure the law is enforced properly will only cost the price of a telephone call and a few postage stamps. There may be cases however when funds are necessary. You might for example need tools for caring for a wood or hedgerow; more trees than your community nursery can provide for planting over a wide area; and you may require fencing or protection for individual trees.

The following sections are a guide to the main sources of grant aid available at local and national levels, and provide suggestions as to how small sums of money might be raised in other ways.

Here are a few general rules to remember when seeking financial help:
- usually, though there are exceptions, you should not start a project or
  incur any expenditure before grant has been awarded
- allow plenty of time for your application to be considered
- do not assume that you will automatically receive the grant or sum
  applied for
- make sure you are applying to the most appropriate body for your project
- ensure that your application is presented in an attractive, clear and
  comprehensive but concise manner.

THE FIRST STOP

When seeking financial help and advice for your tree project you should first contact the district council tree officer or county council countryside officer (usually attached to the planning department). In Wales talk to the Coed Cymru officer based at the county council. They will be able to suggest possible sources of grant aid from statutory bodies for your particular initiative - or at least tell you who to go to for further advice. Many county councils publish their own leaflets or guides to sources of grant aid - ask for one. A large number of county and district councils have their own grant schemes. Some may also provide trees, and sometimes stakes, ties and guards, free of charge to parish councils and amenity groups.

OTHER LOCAL SOURCES

There is a great deal that can be achieved with no money by simply using the experience and talents of local people. Many people will be only too happy to help you with your project without wanting to be paid. A local landholder or farmer may even be willing to lend tools and machinery, if necessary, at little or no cost. Interest your local school and youth groups - they could be a valuable source of enthusiastic labour.

Your local parish (community or town) council might be able to provide financial support for your project. All parish councils are able to spend up to the product of a 2p rate, subject to a few limitations, on anything which is considered by the council to be "in the interests of the area or any part of it, or all or some of its inhabitants". This is known as the 'free two pence'. Dependent on the penny rate product of your parish the amount of money available can range from a few hundred to several thousand pounds. The money is raised by the parish council through its annual rate precept and is commonly used to support local community groups, tree planting and local festivals.

Regional Arts Associations (RAAs) may also be able to provide advice and financial help for trees and woods initiatives which involve the arts - storytelling, photography, music, painting, sculpture. For their addresses write to - The Arts Council of Great Britain, 105 Piccadilly, London W1V 0AV (for addresses of RAA's in England); the Scottish Arts Council, 19 Charlotte Street, Edinburgh, EH2 4DF; or Welsh Arts Council, Museum Place, Cardiff, CF1 3NX.

Local businesses and trusts are also worth approaching for small sums of money - for example to cover equipment costs. The 'Directory of grant-making Trusts' an annual publication by the Charities Aid Foundation, provides details of trusts in your area who might support your work. Consult a copy at your local library. The Directory of Social Change (Radius Works, Back Lane, London NW3 1HL) also produce a number of useful guides to fund-raising and grant-giving trusts - including a leaflet 'Raising Money Locally' (for 50p). Write to them for a copy and a list of other publications.

You could also organise your own fund-raising activities - raffles, competitions, sponsored walks, jumble sales - to gain local support as well as raise money. Profits from a local recycling scheme could be ploughed back into caring for local trees. See 'Holding Your Ground - an action guide to local conservation' by Angela King and Sue Clifford for further ideas on raising money.

NATIONAL SOURCES

There are five main sources of grant aid from national government and agencies for projects concerning trees and woods. These are the Countryside Commission, Nature Conservancy Council, Forestry Commission, the Department of the Environment and the Ministry of Agriculture, Fisheries and Food. Each grant is tailored to a particular type of initiative and rarely is more than one grant available for an individual project. Grants are available for woodland management, hedgerow care, pollarding of willows and alders near rivers and streams, and tree planting in town and country. Special grants for tree care are available in some designated areas - such as Environmentally Sensitive Areas. Your district council tree officer or county council planning department will be able to give you more information about the schemes described in this section; any special grants available in your area and they may be able to supply application forms.

There are a number of other national sources of grant aid for initiatives involving trees and woods. The Tree Council have a budget for supporting tree planting initiatives particularly in urban areas. The Men of the Trees will also provide a small grant for projects it considers to be of particular merit. The BTCV and UK2000 also provide grants towards tree planting initiatives. If your initiative involves wider benefits for the surroundings you might consider applying for support from the more general conservation grant and award schemes, such as the Shell Better Britain Campaign (England and Wales - Red House, Hill Lane, Great Barr, Birmingham, B43 6LZ (021 358-0744); Scotland - Balallan House, 24 Allan Park, Stirling FK8 2QG); the Ford European Conservation Awards and the Trusthouse Forte Community Chest (for details of both schemes contact The Conservation Foundation, 1 Kensington Grove, London SW7 2AR). Shell Better Britain Campaign produce a useful free booklet, 'Getting Help for Community Environmental Projects' - write to them for a copy.

Trees in Schools and Churchyards - The NCC run a grants scheme for School nature areas and from April, 1989, grants will be available for projects which maintain and enhance nature conservation in churchyards (further information from NCC Grants Section in Peterborough).

Grants of around £250 are given to schools wanting to create, use and manage school nature areas. The money can be used to create ponds, establish small wooded areas and hedgerows, and also go towards cost of necessary tools. Application forms are available from the NCC Grants Section and must be returned to your Local Education Authority adviser with responsibility for environmental education.

Recycling - Waste Watch, based at the National Council for Voluntary Organisations, has recently launched a small grants scheme through the Shell Better Britain Campaign for recycling projects for local voluntary groups. Write to them for details. The Department of Environment provide money through local councils under the Urban Programme which might be used for recycling projects. Talk to your local council Recycling or Waste Disposal Officer to find out if money might be available for your local project - either through the Urban Programme or from other sources.

Care for individual or groups of trees - The Countryside Commission can provide a grant for the maintenance of important landmarks, such as hilltop tree clumps and avenues of trees. They will also grant-aid the pollarding of willows and alders in wet areas.

Grants are available to cover a proportion of the costs of the maintenance of existing hedges and the establishment of new ones from: the Countryside Commission - where hedgerows are considered to contribute to the landscape; MAFF - where the hedgerows have an agricultural use (under the new Farm and Conservation Grant Scheme); or the Nature Conservancy Council - where the hedgerow is part of a 'site of nature conservation importance'. In each case grants will cover the costs of traditional hedgelaying, but not annual maintenance costs.

Planting trees and small woods - The Countryside Commission provide grants of up to 50% of eligible costs, including labour, cost of trees, stakes, ties and shelters, for landholders wanting to plant areas of up to 1/4 ha (0.6 acres) - including for the screening of farm buildings. Grant is usually available when planting broadleaved shrubs and trees such as oak, field maple and alder. The Countryside Commission may also grant-aid the establishment of a local tree nursery.

In urban areas the Department of the Environment under the Urban Programme can provide grants through the district or borough council for environmental improvements, including tree planting, in some urban areas - in streets, on housing estates and derelict land.

MAFF can also provide grants for the screening of farm buildings - even when this is a condition of planning permission. Under the Farm and Conservation Grant Scheme they can also provide grants for the planting of shelterbelts and windbreaks, of up to 40% of costs, and single trees for shading stock. Higher rates of grant are paid in some upland areas. You can obtain more information about grants available from the local MAFF office or Farm Conservation Adviser (FWAG).

Woodland Management and Planting - Grants for woodland management are available from the Countryside Commission for work aimed at 'prolonging the life of a wood', if less than 1/4 ha (around 0.5 of an acre). Where you are considering an area of more than 1/4 ha, the Forestry Commission run a new Woodland Grant Scheme (which replaced the old Forestry Grant Scheme and Broadleaved Woodland Grant Scheme in 1988).

The Woodland Grant Scheme aims to

increase timber production and to promote the contribution which new woodlands can make to rural employment, to the provision of alternative uses for agricultural land no longer needed for food production and to the enhancement of landscape, recreation and wildlife conservation. It is also designed to encourage restocking and rehabilitation of existing woodlands either by planting or by natural regeneration.

Under the scheme there are provisions to protect ancient woodland and native pinewood areas by replanting or regeneration with appropriate types of tree; higher rates of grant are available for planting of broadleaves and some grant is available for natural regeneration under 20 years old which has not previously been grant-aided. A five year Plan of Operations has to be approved by the Commission before grant is awarded. A booklet describing the scheme is available from the Forestry Commission HQ and application forms can be obtained from the Commission's regional offices.

For any work in woodland whose primary objective is to enhance wild life, the Nature Conservancy Council can provide grants of up to 50% of acceptable costs. Write to them for further details.

MAFF have recently introduced two schemes providing grant aid for farmers who convert agricultural land to woodland. These are the Farm Woodland Scheme and under set-aside policy. Both are conditional upon receiving planting grants from the Forestry Commission under the Woodland Grant Scheme and both are concerned with encouraging the establishment of woodland on arable land or grassland that has been cultivated and reseeded within the last 10 years. There is a choice for farmers between the set-aside scheme which gives grants per hectare for a period of 5 years; and the Farm Woodland Scheme which provides annual payments for between 10 and 40 years depending on the type of wood to be established - '40 years for oak and beech; 30 years for other broadleaves and mixed woodland containing more than 50% broadleaves; 20 years for other woodland and 10 years for coppice'.

In A Nutshell

Booklets and further information about eligibility, how to apply and rates of grant, can be obtained from your local ADAS office (see telephone directory).

Under the new Farm and Conservation Grant Scheme MAFF are providing grant-aid for fencing-off woodland to prevent grazing by livestock and encourage natural regeneration. The cost of stockproof fencing and associated gates and stiles are covered by the grant. This can be used as an alternative but not in addition to, the FC Woodland Grant Scheme.

Purchasing land/woodland - The NCC can also provide grants to trusts for the purchase of sites of national importance for nature conservation.

In special cases the Countryside Commission may provide financial help towards the cost of purchasing land. In addition the World Wide Fund for Nature spend-"90% of the funds raised in support of organisations purchasing areas of land of national importance. The balance of 10% has in the past been applied to one-off management projects very often on sites purchased with our help, research projects which result in direct benefit to conservation and occasionally educational projects."

Further Reading

A variety of leaflets available from the Directory of Social Change, Radius Works, Back Lane, London NW3 1HL.
Angela King and Sue Clifford, 1987, Holding Your Ground, Wildwood House.
Forestry Commission, 1988, Woodland Grant Scheme, leaflet available from local FC offices.
MAFF, Set-Aside, Farm Woodland and Farm and Conservation Grants, leaflets available from local ADAS office.
Shell Better Britain Campaign, 1988, Getting Help for Community Environmental Projects

oak husk and new oak -

GOOD BOOKS

General/History

Clouston, B., and Stansfield, K., Eds, 1981, **Trees in Towns - maintenance and management**, The Architectural Press.
Edlin, H.L., 1956, **Trees, Woods and Man**, Collins
Fairbrother, N., 1972, **New Lives, New Landscapes**, Penguin
Greenoak, F., 1985, **God's Acre**, E.P. Dutton
Hoskins, W.G., 1970, **The Making of the English Landscape**, Pelican
Lamb, R., 1979, **World Without Trees**, Magnum Books
Mabey, R., 1980, **The Common Ground**, Hutchinson
Muir, R. & N., 1987, **Hedgerows - their history and wildlife**, Michael Joseph Ltd.
Peterken, G., 1981, **Woodland Conservation and Management**, Chapman and Hall
Rackham, O., 1986, **The History of the Countryside**, J.M. Dent and Sons
Rackham, O., 1976, **Trees and Woods in the British Landscape**, J.M. Dent and Sons
Stewart, P., 1987, **Growing Against the Grain**, CPRE
Thomas, K., 1983, **Man and the Natural World**, Penguin

Practical

Baines, C., 1985, **How to Make a Wildlife Garden**, Elm Tree Books
Beckett, K. and G., 1979, **Planting Native Trees and Shrubs**, Jarrold and Sons
BTCV, 1982, **Woodlands - a practical conservation handbook**, BTCV
Emery, M., 1986, **Promoting Nature in Cities and Towns**, Croom Helm Ltd.
King, A., and Clifford, S. for Common Ground, 1987, **Holding Your Ground - an action guide to local conservation**, Wildwood House
Liebscher, K., 1987, **Tree Nurseries**, BTCV
Mitchell, A., 1974, **A Field Guide to the Trees of Britain and Europe**, Collins
Mitchell, A., 1981, **The Gardener's Book of Trees**, J.M. Dent and Sons
Phillips, R., 1978, **Trees in Britain**, Pan Books
Task Force Trees, 1988, **Action Pack** Countryside Commission
Wilkinson, G., 1985, **Woodland Walks**, Ordnance Survey

Trees and Culture

Common Ground & Crafts Council, 1989, **Out of the Wood** - Exhibition Newspaper
Cook, R., (1976), **The Tree of Life - image for the cosmos**, Thames and Hudson
Fowles, J., and Horvat, F., 1979, **The Tree**, Aurum Press
Frazer, J.G., 1987, **The Golden Bough**, Papermac
Giono, J., 1985, **The Man Who Planted Trees**, Chelsea Green Publishing Company
Graves, R., 1961, **The White Goddess**, Faber and Faber
Grigson, G., 1975, **The Englishman's Flora**, Paladin
Hardy, T., 1981, **The Woodlanders**, Penguin
King, A., and Clifford, S. for Common Ground, 1989, **Trees Be Company - an anthology of poetry**, Bristol Classical Press
Mabey, R., King, A., and Clifford, S., 1989, **Second Nature**, Jonathan Cape

South Bank Centre, (1989), **The Tree of Life** - exhibition catalogue, S.B.C.
Taplin, K., 1989, **Pity the Tree - a teacher's guide through woods in children's literature**, Common Ground
Taplin, K., 1989, **Tongues in Trees**, Green Books

Fruit Trees

Greenoak, F., 1983, **Forgotten Fruit**, Andre Deutsch
Hills, L.D., 1984, **The Good Fruit Guide**, Henry Doubleday Research Association
Roach, F., 1985, **The Cultivated Fruits of Britain**, Basil Blackwell
Baker, H., 1986, **The Fruit Garden Displayed**, RHS
Sanders, R., 1988, **The English Apple**, Phaidon

Trees and Pollution

Dowdeswell, W.H., 1987, **Hedgerows and Verges**, Allen and Unwin
Dudley, N., 1985, **The Death of Trees**, Pluto
Pearce, F., 1987, **Acid Rain - what it is and what it's doing to us**, Pengiun
King, K.A. & Ashmore, M.R., 1987, **Acid Rain and Trees**, Nature Conservancy Council

Tropical Rainforests

Caufield, C., 1985, **In the Rainforest**, Picador
Myers, N., 1985, **The Primary Source**, Norton Paperback
Secrett, C., 1985, **Rainforest**, Friends of the Earth

TREES BE COMPANY

Trees Be Company is an anthology of poetry about trees and woods, edited by Angela King and Sue Clifford for Common Ground, with a foreword by John Fowles. This sister volume to **In A Nutshell** is published by Bristol Classical Press at £5.95 (+ £1.20 p & p from Common Ground).

> One impulse from a vernal wood
> May teach you more than man;
> Of moral evil and of good,
> Than all the sages can.
> > William Wordsworth

Poetry is littered with references to trees and woods and the spirits that we give them. In our own deciduous world they call the seasons, they live longer and grow bigger than any other creature - they provide feasts for metaphor, symbol, allegory and they allude to secrets of common culture long trapped in their annual rings.

We feel the time is right to put the cultural arguments about trees and woods alongside the scientific, economic and ecological ones. They need our help.

The intention of **Trees Be Company** is to present evidence of our deep cultural need for trees and woods and to inspire people to take care of them. **In A Nutshell** then offers information and ideas on how to practically care for trees.

If we are to combat local pollution, make even the slightest impact on global warming, enjoy our surroundings and share them with many other creatures - we need trees: trees here and trees now. If we are to nourish more than our prosaic needs we need their longevity; their beauty, their generosity. We are tied to the global turn of events not simply through the ecosystem, but by a universal and deeper need for trees with roots in many cultures. Trees stand for nature and culture. We shall stand or fall with them.

There are so many poems which demonstrate our imaginative relationship with trees, our selection has been guided by a desire to show that the present is as rich as earlier times and we feel strongly that the contemporary poets voice should be heard alongside that of the politicians and professional environmentalists, about three-quarters of the poems are of the 20th Century. So many poets have found richness in the theme - we had to restrict our selection to poems written in English (with a few exceptions Welsh, Irish, Old English, Latin). Poets include William Barnes, Wendell Berry, John Clare, Ruth Fainlight, Seamus Heaney, Norman Nicholson, Kathleen Raine, Stevie Smith, Derek Walcott, Andrew Young.

The gathering of so many poems which use trees as vehicles for their own meanderings has uncovered poets immersed in nature and those who would shun such affiliations. We have found mythology and legend, languages of longevity and seasonal revolution, popular politics and the power of places, lost childhood and golden ages gone, prognoses of good or evil, misplaced love, refuge from the world's ills or own's own afflictions, solace and fears, threat and discovery, and most frequent, a lifting of the soul. All evidence is that we talk to the trees and they speak back to us.